Praise for *Working from the Heart*

"It's readable, it flows, it's interesting.... The examples are wonderful."
—Bernard Haldane, Ph.D., author of *Career Satisfaction and Success*

"A valuable new tool for schools, churches, and job counselors."
—Elsa A. Porter, former assistant secretary, United States Department of Commerce

"*Working from the Heart* provides excellent guidance in finding or creating a more meaningful job based on what your heart desires and your budget allows. I highly recommend it!"
—Mary Rugel Santulli, career transition consultant

"Several years ago, Jackie and Sonya's year-long course helped me bring energy and perspective to my company. Now I find that the exercises in this book are helping me through deep, personal vocational searching."
—Samuel Hale, C.E.O., International Resources, Inc.

"[*Working from the Heart*] is solid and well-written.... [It] is especially good for people who are dissatisfied with their work or thinking about changing."
—Hyler Bracey, author of *Managing from the Heart*

"This book, weaving inspiration, common sense, and highly practical suggestions, is as relevant to the college student just starting out as to the adult in mid-stream. I hope colleges will use it. For all the course work, paper writing, and exams that we ask of our students, we fail them if we don't help them to discern what their heart's work is."
—Elizabeth B. Conant, Ph.D., adjunct professor, Department of Biology, Canisius College, Buffalo, New York

"Readers who work with the exercises in *Working from the Heart* have the possibility of discovering the direction in which their own inner beings are encouraging them to venture."
—Elizabeth O'Conner, author of *Search for Silence* and *Cry Pain, Cry Hope*

"Wouldn't it be wonderful to have a wise and loving Mentor to guide us through the emotional, intellectual, and spiritual 'thickets' that keep us from finding joy and meaning in our Work? If you happen to find such a real-live being, you're very lucky; meanwhile, *Working from the Heart* strives to fill the gap by showing how we can BE that Mentor for ourselves and for each other. It's obvious that this guide is presented out of a deep caring, compassion, and respect for humankind."

—Yana Parker, author of *Damn Good Resume Guide*

"At last! A do-it-yourself guide for people who want their work lives to be an expression of their best selves. . . . A wise, caring and heartening book. *Working from the Heart* goes beyond career development; it is a gift to anyone who wants to live more fully."

—Tom Dunne, organization development consultant

"As a high school teacher in an affluent suburb, I find in today's graduating seniors a disheartening tendency to think of careers primarily as a means of having a BMW in the driveway and possession of other material luxuries. *Working from the Heart* provides a thoughtful and practical program to help young people choose career training or select college programs that they will need in order to make a life and not just a living."

—John Heins, high school English teacher, Virginia

Working from
the Heart

Working from the Heart

A GUIDE TO CULTIVATING THE SOUL AT WORK

Jacqueline McMakin
with Sonya Dyer

POTTER'S HOUSE BOOKSERVICE
Washington DC

WORKING FROM THE HEART:
Guide to Cultivating the Soul at Work

Copyright © 1989 by LuraMedia.
Revised edition copyright © 1993
by Jacqueline McMakin and Sonya Dyer.

All rights reserved including the right to reproduce
this book. For brief quotations, attributions to the
authors and the book must be included.

1989 edition published by LuraMedia.

1993 edition published by HarperCollins.

2004 edition published by Potter's House Bookservice.

For information address:
Potter's House Bookservice
1658 Columbia Road NW
Washington DC 20009
202-232-5483
www.PottersHouseBooks.org
booksandgifts@pottershousedc.org

ISBN: 1-928717-14-4

Printed in the United States of America

The Quote That Keeps Us Going

I think most of us are looking for a calling, not a job. Most of us, like the assembly line worker, have jobs that are too small for our spirit. Jobs are not big enough for people.

Nora Watson,
interviewed by Studs Terkel in Working

Contents

Acknowledgments   *ix*

Introduction: Meaningful Work—It *Is* Possible   *1*

How to Use This Book   *5*

EIGHT STEPS TO WORKING FROM THE HEART

    Step 1. Offer GIFTS You Want to Use   *11*

    Step 2. Incorporate MEANING in Work   *35*

    Step 3. Determine How PARAMETERS Shape Choices   *55*

    Step 4. Move Toward VOCATIONAL DREAMS   *73*

    Step 5. Identify PEOPLE to Help   *93*

    Step 6. Find NOURISHMENT for Your Whole Person   *113*

    Step 7. Contribute to an Effective WORK COMMUNITY   *131*

    Step 8. Create Your BEST WORK   *149*

Appendix A. How to Make Money and Do What You Love   *167*

Appendix B. Interviewing for Information:
    What It Is and How to Go About It   *169*

Appendix C. Training Decisions   *175*

Appendix D. The Cure for Burnout: Refueling Your Tank   *181*

Notes   *183*

Suggested Reading   *187*

About the Authors   *191*

Index   *193*

Acknowledgments

Many people had a hand in shaping and supporting the production of this book. Tish Kashani, one of our seminar participants and our first administrative associate, said, "If only I had learned these tools in college, what a difference it would have made!" Her enthusiasm and helpful research skills got us started. Tom McMakin, Jackie's son, then in college, asked us to work with his friends and urged us to write for a broad audience. He had major input on the final drafts. Friend and colleague Rhoda Nary helped shape the first draft. The title was suggested by Barbara Liles.

Elizabeth Conant has believed in our work and offered invaluable support all along. Our administrative associates, Melissa Stricker, Judy Funderburk, and Carol Ott, gave excellent editorial and word processing assistance. Friends and neighbors criticized drafts and offered technical help: Millie Adams, Peter Bankson, Calista DiGiulian, Sally Dowling, Tom Dunne, Buzz and Nancy Gross, Gretchen and Kim Hannon, Susan and Alison Hogan, Martha Jolkovski, Jean Peterson, Mary Claire Powell, Jean Thompson, Valerie Vesser, and Ricci and Dee Waters.

Several experts offered valuable feedback and encouragement. The first is Bernard Haldane, Ph.D., pioneer in career counseling and human resources development. He has inspired so many of us in this field. Others who were consulted are Richard Broholm, consultant; Hyler Bracey and Jack Rosenblum of the Atlanta Consulting Group; William Byron, S.J. of the Woodstock Center; Horace Deets, executive director of the American Association of Retired Persons; Willis Harman, Institute of Noetic Sciences; Lee Richmond, 1992–1993 president of the American Counseling Association; Robert Rosen, president of Healthy Companies; and Mary Rugel Santulli of Drake Beam and Morin, Inc.

Special thanks to our first editor Lura Jane Geiger and her associate, Marcia Broucek, who saw the potential for this book, and to our present editor, Kandace Hawkinson of Harper San Francisco, who provided excellent coaching on the revised edition.

Our husbands, Dave McMakin and Manning Dyer, endured the whole process with good spirits and continual support. Our other children, Peg

McMakin and Larry, Nancy, and Barbara Darby, all lived the vocational issues we were describing and provided insight and examples, as did our seminar participants and friends, whose impressive commitment to the challenge of finding meaningful work sparks our own.

Introduction
Meaningful Work—
It *Is* Possible!

Do you believe there is something more to life than punching a time clock and earning a paycheck? Have you ever wished that your work made more of a difference in the world? Are you searching for a new job, or looking for ways to infuse meaning into the one you have? Are you willing to invest the time and energy necessary to find work that really satisfies?

If so, you are one of many people deciding not simply to hold down a job but to work from the heart.

Across the land, there's plenty of work to be done—kids to be taught with care and creativity, cities to be restored to top working order, energy-efficient vehicles to be built and maintained with integrity.

There's work to be done. And what is needed is work well done—accomplished with spirit, imagination, and commitment. Yet thousands of people are drifting vocationally, discouraged about finding work that satisfies or alienated from the work they have.

If you are one of these people, it may be comforting to know that you are not alone. Talk with a sampling of people on the bus and you'll find many who are burned out, fed up, overworked, and unappreciated on the job.

Although there may be personal reasons for your plight, societal factors play a part as well. Automation, shifting market needs, demographics, and changing world events all conspire to produce a society characterized by

Unemployment—"I can't find work."

Underemployment—"I'm not challenged."

Misemployment—"I'm not suited for what I do."

Disemployment—"I'm not doing something valuable."

If you feel bogged down in your pursuit for meaningful work, there may be several causes, each addressed by this book.

First, you may be laid low by some of the afflictions common in our complex society: fragmentation, powerlessness, and burnout. This book invites you to turn this situation around, to believe that because you want to contribute, you have something valuable to give. It shows how to *focus* your energies on offering your best through work. It helps you rediscover *passion*, the source of powerful work. And it incites you to seek the *nourishment* you need to sustain your commitment to beautiful work.

Second, you may be confused by the number of factors you need to take into account in the quest for meaningful work. To help you sort these out, this book walks you through an eight-step process to create more meaning in the work you do or to find work that more fully satisfies your heart:

1. Offer GIFTS you want to use.
2. Incorporate MEANING in work.
3. Determine how PARAMETERS shape choices.
4. Move toward VOCATIONAL DREAMS.
5. Identify PEOPLE to help.
6. Find NOURISHMENT to sustain.
7. Create an effective WORK COMMUNITY.
8. Contribute your BEST WORK.

These steps represent habits to cultivate throughout your life to fuel your commitment to satisfying work. Some may have more importance now; others may need attention later; but each step has the potential to give you energy, meaning, and direction at any time.

Seen as a whole, these ideas describe work from the heart. *It is labor that uses our gifts, expresses what matters to us, takes into account our practical needs, and enriches the world.*

The dynamic interrelationship among the eight steps is best illustrated through the metaphor of a living, growing tree. Your unique capacities (*gifts*), the ideals you hold dear (*meaning*), and the practical considerations your life presents (*parameters*) are like an interlocking root system, deeply embedded in your own makeup and situation, overlapping and feeding each other. They are what you bring to work from within yourself. By a creative combining of gifts, meaning, and parameters, allowing them to play against and inform each other, it is possible to come up with vocational aspirations (*dreams*) that capture your imagination. Like a tree trunk, these dreams carry outward what you want to offer. To flourish and bear fruit, these dreams need generous amounts of rain and sun (*people* to help, *nourishment* to sustain, and an

Introduction

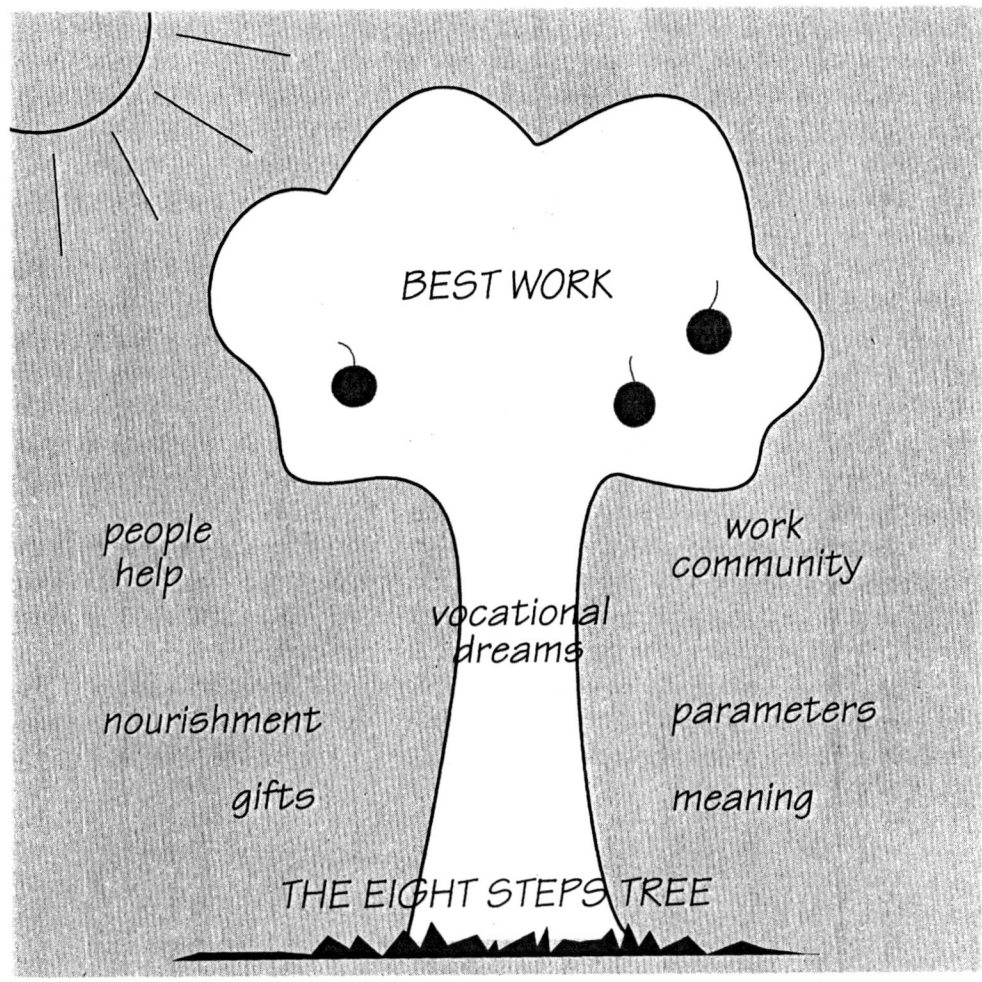

effective work community to support your quest). The fruits that come forth are work opportunities that make excellent use of what you want to offer *(best work)*.

A third reason for being bogged down in your quest for meaningful work is that you may be tired of pursuing it alone. That is why we have included directions and exercises for working with one or more like-minded friends. There is no doubt about it. We do gain energy and support from interaction and feedback.

Fourth, you may find it difficult to program time to find the work you really want to do. That is why this book is organized in bite-sized chunks. A chapter is devoted to each step. Within each chapter are seven numbered segments—if you like, one for each day in a week. Each segment contains a brief reading that can be digested quickly, with suggested exercises to help you apply what you learn. Segments 1 through 5 open up the richness of each step. Segment 6, called Gathering, is a suggested plan to use with others. Segment 7 helps you integrate and apply learnings from the whole chapter.

Throughout the book you will meet people like yourself who want to put more of themselves into work. Although we have changed the names of these people, they are all people we know—our family members, friends, and participants in our seminars. They are bookkeepers, carpenters, executives, teachers, entrepreneurs—people in a variety of occupations at various life stages. We've chosen to include their stories because each story points to a larger truth. You can find something for yourself from each one if you look carefully and do not stop at the outer details of their lives.

The processes and concepts in this book have been distilled from our mentoring experiences with groups and individuals ranging in age from fifteen to eighty. Many of the group processes have been tested in our nine-month Life Direction Labs, offered annually since 1978.

Each of the courageous, committed people we have worked with reinforces our own conviction that meaningful work *is* possible to develop, through enriching the work you have or finding something new. It's worth going after!

      Sonya Dyer   Jacqueline McMakin

How to Use This Book

To decide how you will use this book, recognize and value your present situation. Then respond to these questions:

Will I simply read the book?
You'll receive much.

Will I do the exercises?
You'll receive more.

Will I find a partner to use the book with me?
You'll receive even more.

Will I form a small group with which to use the book?
If you are a person who likes group interaction, this approach can be an especially rich one.

If you are planning to read the book without trying the exercises, go with what attracts you. Some parts of the book may appeal more than others. Let your inclinations lead you.

TIPS FOR DOING THE EXERCISES

Make space. If something new is coming into your life—a new awareness, a different kind of work, a fresh way to do the work you now have—you'll need to make room for it to grow. This is partly a matter of setting aside a special time and place for thinking and dreaming and for doing the exercises.

- Make appointments with yourself; reserve times in your days and weeks to do the suggested exercises. It takes about ten to fifteen minutes to read the segment and from fifteen to sixty minutes to do the activities.

- Set aside a particular place in your office or at home where you can read, write, and ponder.

Assemble your materials. Obtain a looseleaf notebook, a pack of 3 x 5 cards, and a card file box. Use the notebook to record your insights and drawings. On the cards you'll be recording specific content acquired as you do the exercises. Purchase some pencils and pens (colored felt-tips might contribute to your creativity), and keep them reserved especially for this work.

Organize your materials. Get tabs for your notebook and/or file box so you can arrange the discoveries you make in categories. The easiest way to do this is to use the chapter topics for category names. For each chapter, create a Summary Page. A suggested format for these pages is in the illustration on the facing page.

On these Summary Pages you will enter your insights as they occur to you. Use pencil for this so you can readily modify your entries as new insights come.

Cultivate an expectant spirit. You're attracted by the idea of working from the heart. This means that you intend something to happen. Let it.

Bring both your playful and your serious sides to this effort. A combination of commitment and lightness releases creativity. Recent brain research points to ways of liberating creativity by using both sides of the brain: the left side, logical, linear, and rationally oriented, and the right side, where feelings reside, images prevail, and fantasy abounds. The activities in the book encourage both left- and right-brain involvement.

Some suggestions may strike you as odd, or even downright foolish. They aren't. They are intended to help you listen on deeper levels, to get below the conscious, rational, left-brain level and, by doing so, to tap inner sources that are visual rather than verbal. To find work from the heart, every part of you—the child, the clown, the mystic, as well as the planner and thinker—must be fully engaged.

POINTERS FOR WORKING WITH A PARTNER OR A GROUP

Gather kindred souls. Talk with people about your interest in finding work from the heart. You may be surprised by the number of kindred seekers who would like to join you in a disciplined quest. Talk with neighbors, work colleagues, and friends. Invite them to join you. You'll find at least one like-minded partner.

SUMMARY PAGES (suggested format)

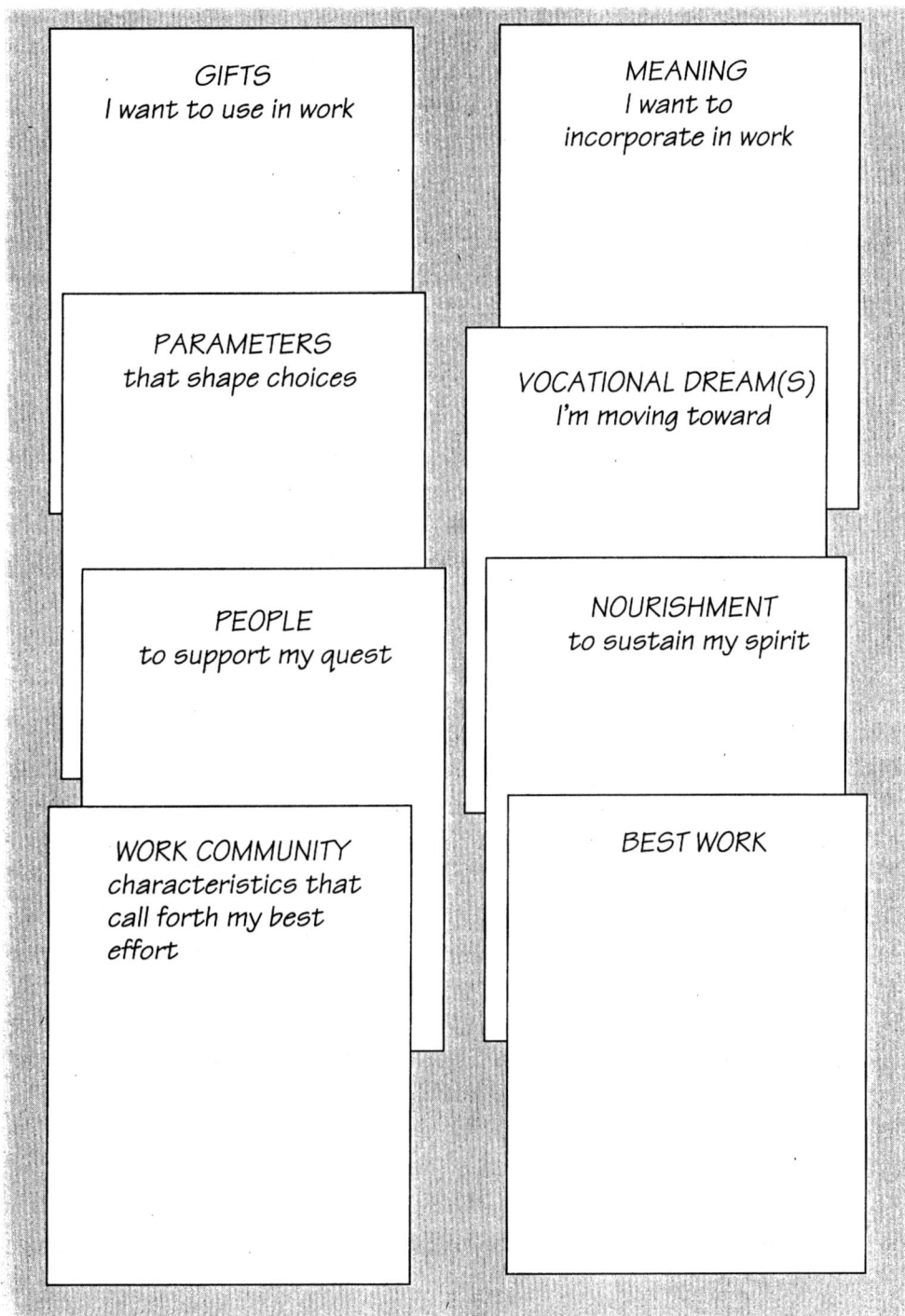

Be clear about specifics. People who want to use this book together in a group need to commit themselves to prepare for and attend each of eight Gathering sessions. Preparations for each session require about two and a half hours (the time needed to do the five half-hour individual exercises that relate to a particular step). Each Gathering session will take about an hour and a half.

Decide how many people to include. You may prefer to work with one other person or to gather a group. The main thing to look for in others is energy and commitment. It's better to have one person who is as motivated as you are about this quest than four others who are not.

Decide on logistics.

- Location of sessions: A home is usually conducive to developing a cohesive group. If you do need to meet in an institutional setting, try to find a spot that is quiet and comfortable.
- Time: Choose a time that works well for everyone so that absences will be minimal.
- Dates: Set dates for all eight sessions at once, and agree to plan around them. This is always a challenge for busy people. Grit your teeth and take the time to do it. You'll be glad you did.

Decide on leadership responsibilities. If you are gathering with just one other person, the two of you can share responsibility for leadership. Groups should decide whether leadership will be rotated or whether the same person or people will convene the group for each session. Here's what the leader or leaders do:

- Read through each Gathering session ahead of time and collect the necessary materials.
- Work out a schedule for each part of the exercise suggested. Consider posting the schedule on newsprint, so that each group member can agree to it and help the group as a whole to stay on track.
- Start the meeting, and outline the agenda.
- If necessary (depending on the size of the group), move the group through the activities, keeping to the agreed-upon timing.
- Help the group to modify the schedule if there are reasons to do so midstream.

How to Use This Book

Even though you have designated leaders, everyone needs to help the group keep on track. Don't sit back. Share, listen, encourage. Help the group stay focused. Together you'll move forward.

Agree on some ground rules. To build momentum and encourage each other, commit to these simple understandings:

- Make all Gatherings a priority.
- If you must be absent, let someone know in advance.
- Be on time. If you have an unavoidable delay, try to let someone know.
- End on time, or agree when you will end.
- Do the individual exercises and readings between Gatherings and come prepared to give and receive.
- Bring all your work to each session.

Make your meetings lively. The following suggestions work well to keep things flowing and fruitful. Consider reading them aloud before each session and reminding each other of them when needed.

- Share what is fresh for you as a result of doing the individual work.
- Don't get bogged down with opinions.
- Engage with others—say a little, let others engage with you. Don't run on forever.
- Share what's most important. Do some sifting.

Remember—the purpose of the Gathering session is to stimulate you to go back to your individual work (where the real pay dirt is) with new gusto. It is not always necessary to finish a discussion or complete a thought. Research shows that unfinished tasks keep creativity going and brain cells churning. If your allotted time for a certain activity is up, leave it unfinished and move on. The goal is to gain insight personally, not to have full sharing.

These suggestions for getting the most from this book are open to your modification as you develop your own best work style. Each idea is worthy of consideration.

Important as the how-tos are—
most important is to begin.

Offer GIFTS You Want to Use

This, I believe, is the great Western truth: that each of us is a completely unique creature and that, if we are ever to give any gift to the world, it will have to come out of our own experience and fulfillment of our own potentialities, not someone else's.
Joseph Campbell

1 A Field Guide to Your Gifts

Most of us know people who work from the heart. They labor with love, their gifts combine with a sense of purpose to produce energy. Malcolm is ninety-one years old. Despite his age, he shows no signs of slowing down. A wood carver, he has a real eye for color. Paint, wood, glitter, and glue crowd the corners and cupboards of his small home. For ten years, Malcolm has been creating handmade toys for school kids, not just around Christmastime, but every day of the year. He is known as the King of Toys.

"I like to make kids happy," he says. Intricate doll furniture, tricky puzzles, colorful wagons, and—best of all—conversations with grateful boys and girls crowd his busy days.

"I work until I get tired or hungry," he says. "Then I stop just long enough to take a nap or eat something, and I start again."

Sarah manages a paint store. The way she does it tells you how much her work means to her. She is hospitable and welcoming; her forthright personality and direct approach help you clarify what you need and find what you want. She knows her products, cares about her customers, and takes great pleasure in seeing the freshly decorated homes that result from her efforts.

Malcolm and Sarah have each found their niche. They demonstrate in living color the power of our first step:

Offer GIFTS you want to use.

This chapter brings this step alive for us. It puts forward these key points: Employ the fullness of your gifts, not simply your skills (Segment 1). Engage your own expertise in naming these gifts and tapping your creativity (Segment 2). Roll up your sleeves and dig for gifts in many places. The "aha" discoveries you make will light your fire (Segment 3). Invite others to help you identify those gifts that have most energy for you now (Segment 4). Put your gifts to work. They'll develop, multiply, and become more useful (Segment 5). Be imaginative about connecting the gifts you want to use with the money you need to earn (Segment 7).

First, consider what we mean by the term *gifts*.

If you think of gifts as "something you're good at," you might have one common reaction, "I'm not sure what my gifts are or even if I have any." Let go, for the moment, of that first instinctive definition. Think instead about *activities you enjoy*—being alone in the woods, appreciating fine craft work, or wrestling with the kids.

Are the "activities you enjoy" really gifts? Sure! Either they are themselves gifts, or they point to gifts. That you enjoy wrestling with the kids, for example, could mean that athletic ability is your gift, or maybe it points to another one—rapport with children.

A gift can be a *personal characteristic*. On the employee relations committee at work, George sparks the group with enthusiasm and buoyancy, whereas Jan tends to be cautious, asking thoughtful questions when a decision has to be made. Both George's enthusiasm and Jan's caution are gifts.

Used more broadly, the term *gift* also includes *personal experience*—good or bad. Harold's heart operations were hardly what anyone would call a gift. However, once a week you find Harold, now recovered, visiting patients in the hospital as part of its Mended Hearts program. He knows what heart patients go through because he has been there himself. Who would have thought that Harold's experience with heart trouble would become a gift he wanted to offer others?

Having a gift does not necessarily mean you have a certain skill or talent. An *appreciation* is also a gift. Jessica has fond memories of singing around the family piano as a child. Now she wants to help her own family enjoy music. She doesn't play an instrument, has never had formal musical training, and, in truth, does not have much musical ability. Rather, her gift is love of music. This she passes on to her family.

With all that said, a *talent or skill* surely is a gift. Our talents don't have to be either fully developed or outstanding to be useful. Skills need not be static. We can grow as we strengthen our skills in areas we find rewarding.

Using this broad view of gifts, you can see that *each of us has a bundle of characteristics, experiences, and skills, as well as things we enjoy and appreciate, that are special to us.* That is what we mean by the term *gifts*.

People like Malcolm and Sarah have learned something important. Creating meaningful work does not consist simply in using a skill we do well, although it includes that. More is involved. It requires offering our totality. Our skills comprise part of what we have to offer. The rest of us—our characteristics and experiences and what we enjoy and appreciate—adds spice, wisdom, color, and brightness to the day.

When we offer the fullness of our gifts, our work does not rob us of energy but gives it to us. The quality of our work increases. The rich mix of who we are is what enables us to innovate, to be creative, to offer our best. These abilities are fed by all the things we have done in life—both the conventional and the unconventional. That's why it's important to pursue all kinds of clues—no matter how crazy or extraneous they might seem—to what we have to offer.

Thus for our own fulfillment, for the benefit of our work, and for the purpose of discerning our particular contribution to others, it is necessary to identify and use our unique endowment—the wonderful spicy mix of all our gifts.

EXERCISE

To get started in thinking about your uniqueness, consider this slightly offbeat question. Write down your responses in your notebook.

> What would you be
>
> if you could be something else?

Use your imagination. If you could be an animal, what animal would you be? If you could be a color, a car, a flower, a place—what would you be?

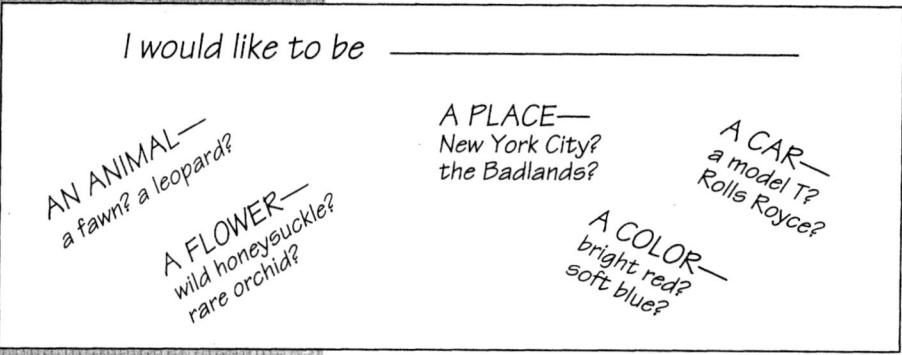

Now go back and ask yourself why you chose what you did. Reflect on what your choices tell you about special qualities or gifts you might have.

Susan found herself thinking that she'd like to be a bright red Corvette convertible. Why? "I like red," she offered simply. "It's dynamic, fiery, full of life! And the Corvette is a true classic. I also like the idea of being open to the wind and weather." As she thought more about her choice, Susan realized that she was describing qualities she liked in herself—her dynamism, her sense of freedom, even her "classiness."

Write down the names of the qualities or gifts you have discovered in doing this exercise. These are enjoyable parts of yourself. Which could you bring into play at your work now or in your search for work?

Important tip: The exercise above and each of the following ones is more fun and productive to do if you invite at least one other person to join you. Bounce ideas, impressions, and insights off each other. Egg each other on. Be a little wacky in the process. You'll come away with a variety of perspectives on your gifts.

2 You Are the Best Expert

In our seminars, when we invite people to embark on the adventure of discovering more about their gifts, often we see frightened looks. Why is this? Here are some of the responses we hear:

"I'm afraid I don't have any gifts."

"I wanted to sing in the school chorus, and the leader said I was tone deaf. I felt put down, squelched."

"Dad and Mom said not to brag, so I learned to hide those things that made me feel proud."

"If I find out I have a certain gift, then I'll be responsible for making good use of it. That's scary."

You might have similar feelings. They're like evil green-haired trolls lurking in the deep recesses of our minds, whispering, "Don't do it. You'll fail. How dare you?" These little devils got into our system at an early age. Now it's time to grab them by the scruff of the neck and let them know they are not welcome. You have work to do.

Allow another image to take their place. Imagine that you are a gifted potter with a generous piece of moist clay in your hands. You have a mental image of a gorgeous pitcher you would like to create. You throw the clay on the wheel, gently guiding the shape you imagine. Suddenly, the sides of your embryonic vessel collapse. You have exerted a bit too much pressure, or the clay is too dry. Something is wrong. You analyze the cause of collapse. Then you begin again. You know you may need to repeat the throw many times before the pitcher takes the shape you wish. Even then, it will not conform exactly to what you imagine. It has its own life. You understand this because you are an artist. You recognize that mistakes and failures are part of the process. They can be your teachers.

Now turn back to yourself. Even though your native creativity might have been dampened by harsh treatment in the past, it can be awakened by sensitive cultivation now. We awaken our creativity when we adopt the attitudes and actions native to highly creative people. These are described by the artist Lois Robbins in her book *Waking Up in the Age of Creativity*.[1]

Creative people are willing to fail, notes Robbins. They expect it. To discover what does not work is part of the experimentation required in the process of finding out what does.

Creative people cultivate "beginner's mind," the ability to bring to projects a fresh approach, a childlike innocence, the recognition that they have much to learn. They don't have to know it all before they try.

Creative people are playful. They don't have to "do it right"; they just enjoy doing it. Unafraid of looking silly, they thrive on being different. Robbins writes, "Free, happy 'fooling around' can result in new connections which often suggest the most creative solutions to problems."[2]

Creative people feed their fantasy, sensory, and emotional life. A painter surrounds herself with beautiful art, all kinds of colors and brushes. Creative people make sure that they do not suffer from what Robbins calls "resource myopia," which is "the failure to see one's own strengths and the resources around one."[3]

Most important, creative people understand that the creative process is full of ups and downs, frustrations and breakthroughs. Inspiration causes the birth of a new idea. The light bulb goes on. But it is with *perspiration* that the image is pushed through to full expression in a completed artwork.

No matter how much the devilish green trolls might have undermined your confidence in your own giftedness, you are still the best expert on what you really love to do and to be. Your latent capacities are not lost; they still exist in the creative, playful, childlike parts of yourself. To tap your expert knowledge, adopt the stance of the open-hearted artist. Put aside efforts to direct into predictable categories what you love to do or be. Let other parts of yourself emerge.

Offer GIFTS You Want to Use   17

EXERCISE

Don't *work* at the following activities. Let your spontaneity guide you.

■ Draw a simple sketch of yourself. Identify what you love doing with various parts of your body: head, ears, mouth, hands, legs, feet, heart, and so on.

When John, one of our seminar participants, did this, he drew the following:

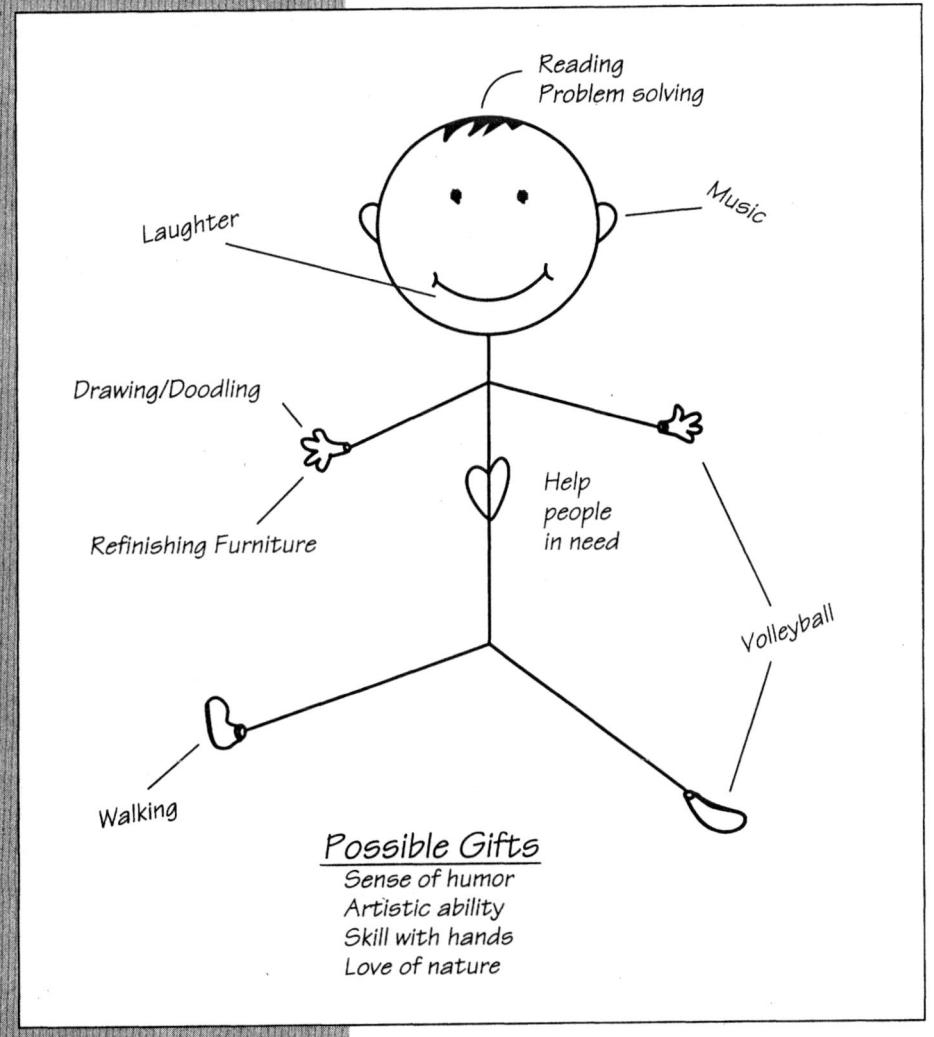

■ Look at your sketch and think about what gifts are involved in each activity. Write down each gift you identify.

■ Tapping into childhood memories helps you get in touch with long-buried gifts; adult ways of thinking can actually keep those gifts buried. To bypass habitual modes of thought, experiment in this exercise with using your *nondominant* hand to do the writing. This will help you remember lesser-known or forgotten parts of yourself.

Get a pencil and your notebook ready. Then take a moment to relax and be still inside. Sit back and remember what it was like to be twelve years old. Get in touch with what you were really like—the real you, not just the surface you who behaved as teachers or parents wished. As the sense of yourself at twelve takes hold, pick up your pencil and write your name with your nondominant hand. Then write a sentence as your twelve-year-old self. Who are you? What are you like? Expand this sentence to a paragraph. Follow your hand, and let yourself speak from a different, perhaps more primitive, place than you do with ordinary conscious thinking.

Now take a look at what you've written. Switch your pencil to your dominant hand and continue writing about who you, as a twelve-year-old, want to be when you "grow up."

Getting in touch with what you loved as a child may help you rediscover some gifts that you have forgotten. Reflect on what you have written, and list the gifts revealed through your trip back in time.

3 Dig for Treasure

The stories of how our gifts develop reveal a great deal about the fascinating process of identifying the gifts we have and want to use. As examples, we'll look at Fran's love of music and Mario's gift for cultural diversity. We'll see that searching for gifts is like digging for treasure—the more places you look, the more you find.

Picture Fran as a curious four-year-old clamoring for piano lessons. She loved her practice periods. No matter how well or poorly she played, her mother frequently said, "I love to hear you practice."

A few years later, Fran begged for violin lessons in addition to her piano work. Her parents, thinking they had a musical genius on their hands, began imagining a future for Fran in solo performance. That was the only outlet they could think of for what seemed to them a strong gift. Seeking advice on her prospects, they took her to a well-known conductor in the city. Upon hearing the few shaky squeaks produced from her fiddle and observing her piano playing, the conductor said, "I can see her enthusiasm, but I don't see great musical talent."

Undaunted, Fran continued to practice on the piano. One day, as a sixth grader, in the midst of performing a difficult Chopin waltz before four hundred kids in the school assembly, she suddenly went blank and could not continue. Running from the assembly to her home not far away, she sobbed, "I'm never going to play piano again. What happened was so awful!"

Refusing to do any more solo performances, she still enjoyed band, orchestra, and chorus right through high school. During that time she took some vocational testing that revealed helpful information: she scored high in pitch recognition and personal interactive capacity but low in finger dexterity. A wise counselor pointed out that although she had some musical ability, her love of people would prevent her from spending the six hours in daily practice needed for solo performance. Fran recognized the truth in this. Thus, in college she decided to prepare for the field of music education, something that combined her love of music and people. Once again, however, she was told that her performance ability was not strong enough.

Years later, she took a temporary job teaching music at a school for learning disabled children. There she found a satisfying outlet for her medium-level musical gifts. Bringing instruments for the kids to try, simplifying musicals for them to perform, and gently coaxing impaired students to express themselves, Fran was in her element.

From Fran's story we can see the complexity and subtlety of identifying our gifts and ways to use them. The exact nature of Fran's gift was not easy to identify. Her parents first called it "solo performance." After the vocational testing, Fran began to think of it as "music teaching." In her temporary job, she liked to say the gift she shared with students was a love of "fooling around with music." Several years later, when invited to think of an image that seemed to depict the energy of her life, what popped into her mind was "music making." That rang true as a description for Fran. Her awareness had broadened. Not only did she enjoy musical activity, especially with others, but she delighted in deepening her appreciation of the music of life.

From Fran's experience we see how impossible it is to freeze the process of gift identification. It is evolving and dynamic.

Also we see that others, not only Fran, contributed to her awareness. Her mother's early appreciation reinforced Fran's own love of music. Even her parents' misguided picture of Fran's gift as solo performance led eventually to Fran's recognition that this was not for her. Vocational testing shed useful light on her discernment process but was by no means definitive.

We notice also that there were a number of shifts in Fran's use of her gift. Sometimes it was a prime ingredient of professional work and at other periods an avocational pursuit.

Further, Fran's gift did not have to be outstanding to be useful. However, it did require ingenuity on her part to find a setting where her medium-level ability truly was an asset.

Her gift has brought much joy, but there has been struggle too. Not only has Fran found it tough to make peace with her limited talent, it has been hard to cope with the times when using it has produced frustration or hurt.

We used Fran's musical gift as an example because it is so tangible. Unlike Fran, Mario wondered whether he had any gifts at all. The middle child in a large family, he tended to blend in; it was easier that way. His father, often absent with his sales job, cracked down on discipline when at home. Meanwhile, his mother barely kept up with the kids, the housework, and her job.

Later he wrote this about his childhood:

> Though I found peace and adventure outdoors, I faced fear, fury, and cutting silence within the house. I hated it there. I whispered when I played, checked every thought and move before I spoke or acted. I learned how to try to be invisible. My metaphor of success was to enter into an existing circle of people without making anyone else move. This is when I learned to walk away from myself. My energy, enthusiasm, and spunk dropped off inside, even though I was outwardly very energetic and successful.

Mario's solace was to walk alone in his inner-city neighborhood. Observing other kids and their families, he silently recorded how people lived together. He was fascinated with the community where he lived. Italians rubbed elbows with Puerto Ricans. Asians, African Americans, and Caucasians mingled freely. Mario realized it was like a little United Nations.

This experience planted in him a lifelong appreciation for diversity. As a young adult, he helped design an inner-city Head Start program that served youngsters of many backgrounds. As director of that program, he brought his own child to its classes. Together they experienced people of different races, educational levels, economic means. This experience was enriching for them both, but it was also tough when cultural differences caused tension for Mario and his four-year-old daughter.

Over the years, Mario continued to carry his gift for breaking down barriers between people. It was not until recently, however, that he was able to influence the company where he now works to seek more diversity at all levels of employment. As a manager of an increasingly diverse work force, Mario finds ways to emphasize the incredible richness that results when people embrace their differences.

Mario's gift, a respect for diversity, has found expression in work, family life, and the community, but not always as fully as he would wish. Moreover, it was sometimes costly to express. However, it is so much a part of him that he takes every chance he gets to experience and share its blessings.

Through these stories about Fran and Mario, we have a picture of how gifts are often more than what immediately meets the eye, of how they evolve and are expressed in a variety of ways over time. When we do the hard work of sifting through our experience in a search for gifts, we find treasure.

Joan Smith, a career development consultant, says, "We all need to do a lot of exploring and experimenting to define our gifts. Many of us think we are supposed to know all this when we leave school, or that there is nothing new to find out about our talents after that. Not so! Keep looking and listening . . . and don't ever stop."[4]

EXERCISES

Now let's focus on you. What follows is a cornucopia of places to search and ways to identify gifts. Look them over. Choose one or more that appeal now. Be on the lookout for chances to explore the others as you have the time and inclination.

   1. As we did with Fran and Mario, write the story of a gift you have. Notice how it changes and develops. How would you describe it now?

- or -

   2. Take a moment to write down the names of two people you have always admired—one living, one dead. Write the name of a book, play, or movie that you count as a favorite. And finally, jot down the name of an event—perhaps a wedding, a speech, or a concert—that has always stuck in your mind.

Pick one of the people you chose. Imagine sitting down with this person in your living room and sharing a cup of tea. Start an imaginary conversation, describing the reasons you admire the person. Now envision the person saying, "Thanks so much for telling me these things. But, you know, I think your admiration points to interests, skills, and experiences that you have to offer. I think you too are . . ." Write down what the person tells you.

Repeat this for the second person you picked.

Now—since you're getting better at talking with ghosts—imagine engaging the director of your favorite movie or play or the author of your favorite book in a similar conversation. What does he or she have to tell you about your gifts?

Finally, imagine you are speaking with the organizer of the event you enjoyed. Does she or he tell you something about your gifts?

Write down the names of the gifts you have discovered in doing these exercises.

As Carol did this exercise, she thought about Eleanor Roosevelt, a woman she had always admired. "Let's see," she mused, "what do I like about her? I know . . ." Then she spoke to Eleanor, "I've always been impressed with how you triumphed over limitation, how you took a positive stand even when it was not popular, and how you have been an advocate for the oppressed." Then Carol become quiet and imagined Eleanor speaking to her, "Carol, you have overcome many obstacles in your life. You are a strong woman. And your heart reaches out to people having a hard time. In conversations, you defend people in weaker positions. How can you make these traits a part of what you do at work?"

- or -

3. Look around your home and select four or five favorite pieces you have collected—a vase, a photo or picture, perhaps a natural object—those things you count as treasures. Pick one up, take some time to examine it afresh. Remember why you chose it in the first place. Then jot down what you appreciate about it. These appreciations are gifts. Repeat with another object, if you wish. Let it speak to you about your unique taste and perception.

4 Let Others Help You Discover Your Bliss

Have you seen the bumper sticker that says, "Follow your bliss"? This phrase describes the path Joseph Campbell took to discover his life's purpose. Unable to find a job during the depression, the young medieval literature graduate took to the woods. As he tells it, "My father had lost all his money but I had saved some as a student. I used to play in a jazz band and so I piled up money during a few years. And on that, you might say, I just retired to read, and read, and read, and read, for *five* years. No job, no money. . . . Reading what you want, and having one book lead to the next, is the way I found my discipline."[5]

Many years later, interviewer Bill Moyers asked Joseph Campbell, then a renowned mythology scholar, what he meant by following your bliss. How do you know what makes you truly happy? Campbell replied, "The way to find out about your happiness is to keep your mind on those moments when you feel most happy, when you really are happy—not excited, not just thrilled, but deeply happy. This requires a little bit of self-analysis. What is it that makes you happy? Stay with it, no matter what people tell you. This is what I call 'following your bliss.'"[6]

The pioneer career counselor Bernard Haldane articulated the same truth in a different way. He put forward a profound but deceptively simple truth: what we enjoy we do well. The people he knew who were truly happy in their jobs had found a way to be paid for doing what they love. They employed those gifts they were motivated to use. Equally important is to do what we believe in, even though we may have moments that are not enjoyable.

The place to look for what we enjoy and believe in is in those experiences when we have felt truly alive, times that in retrospect we would call *good*. Dr. Haldane invented an exercise that we use in slightly modified form to look at these experiences for clues to what we really enjoy, do well, and value. It entails describing a good experience to one or more people, who then help us name the gifts it reveals. Here's an illustration of how it works. In one of our seminars, Julia spoke to the group about this delightful memory.

> It happened in the summer, when I was visiting my grandfather's farm in western Maryland. I used to love getting my cousin to dress up with me. We'd go up in the attic, pull out long black dresses and hats, and put them on, with gloves and jewelry. We looked terrific!

Then we'd knock at the front doors of neighbors' houses, and say, "Could you please tell us where William Wallace's house is?" (This, of course, was my grandfather!) The neighbors would play along with us. They'd give us directions and then bid us a warm farewell.

One seminar participant asked, "What was so appealing about this experience?"

Julia thought a moment. "We loved how we looked. And it was so much fun to pretend."

"How did you feel when you did that?" asked another participant.

"Oh, we felt so grown-up and important!" Julia replied.

After a few more minutes of exchange, people in the group started identifying what they thought were Julia's strengths and gifts. "You have the gift of imagination," said one.

Julia's eyes brightened. "Yes, that's right. I think I do."

"And I think you are theatrical!" said another.

"Well, I've never quite thought of myself that way, but I guess you're right," replied Julia.

"What about the gift of being in charge?" contributed another person.

Julia pondered a bit. "No, I'm not sure that's quite it. My cousin was older, and I was younger. I don't remember instigating these dress-up sessions. Rather, we cooked them up together. We egged each other on."

"Oh," said another participant. "Perhaps your gift is creating together."

"Yes," replied Julia, becoming more animated. "That's it. I love doing that."

In five minutes, the group helped Julia confirm these possible gifts: imagination, playfulness, theatricality, creating together, being a co-conspirator, working as part of a team, entertaining, being able to find another who complements you, the ability to recruit allies, being able to draw people out, presence, communicating through appearance, appreciation of physical image.

You get the idea by now of how to do our version of Dr. Haldane's exercise. It involves listening and being attentive. You're on a hunt for energy, noticing what turns the other person on or lights their fire. It's important not to fix too quickly on the exact identity of a gift. Take time to fine-tune it so that a more precise and energizing name may emerge.

In a very real sense, when we help each other identify gifts, we act as mentors for each other, calling forth and affirming our strengths and capacities. Frequently, the term *mentor* is used to describe an "up-down" relationship, the experienced worker coaching the newcomer. For our purposes, the term *mutual mentoring* is useful. No matter what position we hold in our fam-

Offer GIFTS You Want to Use

ily or organization, we can all mentor one another in naming and then making full use of gifts.

Get others to help you identify your gifts. They see your potential with fresh eyes. Unaware of any discouragement or fear you might feel, other people bring an imagination, spirit, interest, and enthusiasm that you might not have when contemplating your own gifts.

Mutual mentoring is a powerful activity and attitude to bring to our families, workplaces, and communities to call forth excellence. Let's get going and prepare to do this.

EXERCISE

What is your "bliss"? Think about those moments when you have been "deeply happy," when you have felt you were really yourself, your best self—when you have felt most alive. These moments are "good experiences." Your good experiences may or may not have anything to do with work. And they are not dependent on other people's assessment, only your own. According to Dr. Haldane, good experiences are the things that "you feel you have done well, have enjoyed doing, and that have given you deep satisfaction"—the things that you felt expressed "the real you."

If examples do not come readily to mind, be still, and make room for impressions and wisps of thought that may come into your mind on their own. Remember, you are the decider. Your good experiences are not necessarily those that have been recognized or valued by others.

Over time, make a list of twenty "good experiences." To do this, divide your life into four quarters, age-wise. For each quarter list five good experiences.

On page 26 are four of the twenty good experiences that John listed (one for each quarter).

This exercise is not easy for everyone to do. Listen to Laura's account of her process:

> At first, I thought this would be easy. On the contrary, it was quite difficult. Not so much the earlier, childhood years or my twenties or early thirties. The real difficulty started with my middle years—my "barren" period, as I call it—when I not only stagnated but very nearly lost all my self-respect and self-confidence. However, several days later, after I had already finished this assignment, more and

> **MY GOOD EXPERIENCES**
>
> - *concocting pranks at summer camp (age 8)*
>
> - *regaining motor ability after sports accident (age 20)*
>
> - *being a friend to my teenaged daughter (age 38)*
>
> - *acting in the community theater group (age 50)*

Good Experiences in My Life

1st quarter (age   to   )   *2nd quarter (age   to   )*

_____   _____

_____   _____

_____   _____

_____   _____

_____   _____

3rd quarter (age   to   )   *4th quarter (age   to   )*

_____   _____

_____   _____

_____   _____

_____   _____

_____   _____

> more past experiences surfaced and made me feel better even about those middle years. I hope that I am on my way to an even better period and that I might be able to develop those hidden gifts that must be buried deep inside me.
>
> Laura's remarks highlight several points about how to go about doing this activity. Give yourself enough time. Do it at one sitting if that is best for you, or jot down your good experiences whenever they occur to you.
>
> Some periods in your life might yield several good experiences and others might have few. Do find some for each quarter, even if you have to consult someone who knew you during a particular period to jog your memory. Experiences in your early life, especially, reveal parts of you that may have been lost or hidden as you grew and took on more of the expectations of others.

Give Your Gifts a Workout

Don't wait for a far-off future to bring your gifts out from hiding. Gifts are like muscles. The more you use them, the stronger they become. Use gifts today and every day. Your ability will expand, you'll grow as a person, and you'll have more to contribute to your work. Using gifts pours significance into what you do no matter what situation you're in.

Gifts shape work. As a youngster, Brian did not feel he was good at anything. He found otherwise in three decades at Mobil Oil Corporation. Over the years Brian has offered talents and developed skills that have helped move his organization forward at critical times. First, he provided needed management experience learned at another company. Next, during the oil embargoes of the 1970s, he provided expertise in regulatory affairs. Currently, Brian brings a broad background to his responsibility for delivery of crude oil to refineries. He feels intense satisfaction from doing his work well. Says Brian, "It means a lot when others recognize that I know what I'm doing, but it means much more that I know I'm good at what I do." By consistently using and developing a variety of gifts, Brian positioned himself to gain increasingly challenging jobs within his company.

Gifts provide direction for work change. As a high school English teacher, Kathryn shared with students her love of language, her gift of writing, her ability to call forth students' potential. However, to spend more time with her own young children, she decided to leave her teaching position, which required long hours. Wondering how her facility with words could be used in her own home business, she spoke with a friend whose work involved soliciting charitable gifts. An idea occurred to her: write fund-raising letters for organizations whose causes she believes in. The love of language and gift for writing that Kathryn had used in teaching now find a new use in her profitable direct-mail marketing business.

Gifts refresh work. Sam, a senior analyst in the Census Bureau, is an able statistician who enjoys crunching numbers. Gourmet cooking also gives him special delight. When a particularly thorny problem was to be discussed at the next staff meeting, Sam brought in his favorite fresh-baked cookies. That got the meeting off to a good start! To spice up her work, Verna dashes off zany memos to her colleagues. Millie and Emily enjoy rounding up work mates for an after-hours volleyball game. Certain gifts, though not central to our work, add zest to what we do.

Even if you don't think you have distinctive gifts, all of us, by virtue of our humanity, have gifts in common. One is the gift of the soul, or heart—our unique spirit. It often takes just a touch—a gift of flowers, a cartoon, a quick note, a smile—to bring spirit to life. When we ground what we do in the human heart and not just in the brain, our work becomes a labor of love, according to the therapist Thomas Moore.[7] This happens when we bring attention, standards, imagination, pride, grace, spontaneity, and even artfulness and passion to what we do.

When we withhold the gift of soul from work, the consequences are serious. According to Moore, "If what we do or make is not up to our standards, and does not reflect attention and care when we stand back to look at it, the soul suffers. The whole society suffers a wound to soul if we allow ourselves to do bad work."[8]

Care and compassion are attributes of soul that all of us can offer at any time. They are every bit as important as bottom-line productivity. If we kill the spirit of colleagues through lack of care, nothing much matters. In their arresting parable *Managing from the Heart*, the authors had some fun with the character Harry Hartwell, a blustery oil executive who manages people by scaring them half to death. Felled by a heart attack, his recovery depends on a major behavioral turnaround. He must learn to manage from the heart, or it's curtains for him! Principles for heart management are contained in the acronym (you guessed it!) HEART:

Hear and understand me.

Even if you disagree, don't make me wrong.

Acknowledge the greatness within me.

Remember to look for my loving intentions.

Tell me the truth with compassion.[9]

Wow! What a difference from the way he usually operated! These caring principles rest on the assumption that we and our colleagues are doing the best we can with what we have been given. Harry Hartwell had a terrible time believing this, especially about his rivals. Kicking and screaming, he changed his attitude and behavior and learned a priceless truth in the process: when our feelings are understood and our ideas valued, we feel like part of a team and do our best to make our organization prosper.

The gifts of heart, soul, care, and compassion, common to us all, add much to what we do. Our distinctive gifts add even more. The more we use our gifts, the stronger they become. That increases our confidence. We're then willing to step out more boldly. Certainly, there are times we cannot see how our gifts fit, or we recognize that they need more development before they are fully useful. That is to be expected. Yet the more focused we are on the gifts we truly want to use at work, the more likely we will find opportunities large and small to use those gifts.

> **EXERCISE**
>
> Look over all the gifts you've identified so far. Choose one that you'd like to use more fully at work.
>
> Write that gift on a 3 x 5 card. Using colored pens, decorate your card with flourishes or shapes or forms. Giving attention to your gift in this way reinforces your intention to use it. Put your card in your work space. Throughout the day, seek opportunities to use this gift. Note each time you did so on the back of your card.
>
> If this reminder system works for you, create another card for a different gift. Decorate that. Then employ that one throughout the day, noting instances when you did so.

> A variation on this theme: note one aspect of your work that seems like drudgery to you. Scan your list of gifts. Which would bring some life to that boring part of your job? Be intentional about offering that gift to this part of your work. Note what happens.

Gathering

Purpose: To help each other discover and name gifts
Leaders bring: Newsprint, magic markers, pencils, paper
Everyone bring: Good Experiences in My Life from Segment 4

WARM-UP (EVERYONE)
15 MINUTES

Share with your partner or group one discovery about gifts—an insight from the reading or something you have learned about your own gifts.

DISCOVER GIFTS TOGETHER (IN TWOS)
60 MINUTES

Here are the directions for the process Julia engaged in. You might want to review her story before you begin.

1. Work in pairs. Decide who will act first as Sharer and who will be the Listener.
2. The Sharer describes a favorite experience from the list Good Experiences in My Life.
3. The Listener asks questions to help the Sharer elaborate. As the Sharer says more, the Listener writes notes about the gifts that he or she is noticing in the description.
4. Repeat steps 2 and 3 as many times as possible within twenty minutes.

5. When twenty minutes are up, the Listener names the gifts that he or she has noted and gets the Sharer's response to the gifts just identified, and together they refine the list.
6. Then the Listener writes a list of the gifts that both partners have recognized and gives it to the Sharer.
7. Reverse the process so that the Listener becomes the Sharer and the Sharer the Listener. (Be sure to budget half your time for each person. It is disappointing if a disproportionate amount of time is used to name gifts for one person.)

HOW IT WENT (EVERYONE)
10 MINUTES

Popcorn (that is, do a spontaneous, easy, flowing kind of sharing that builds on each person's offerings) how it was to be the Sharer and the Listener. Talk about what you learned and what you felt during the process.

CLOSING (EVERYONE)
5 MINUTES

Be sure to close the session in a way that creates a feeling of unity and completion, whether you are working in pairs or in a group.

Gather in a circle and share one or more of the following:

- Words of appreciation of what happened
- Ideas to make the next session more effective
- Insights gained
- Support needed for the next step
- A motivating reading or thought
- Silence

Note: Subsequent Gathering sessions will indicate simply "Closing." Refer back to these suggestions if necessary. The point is to create a closing ritual that particularly suits your group.

7 How Will the Money Follow?

The title of Marsha Sinetar's best-selling book *Do What You Love, The Money Will Follow* suggests a crucial question. If I use the gifts I enjoy, can I make the money I need?

The answer is "Yes, if . . ." If you're willing to work hard, be patient, and open yourself to a variety of ways it could work out. Both Gail, a woman in her fifties, and Nathan, in his thirties, were resourceful in how they matched financial requirements with gifts they wanted to use.

As the wife of a foreign service officer, Gail has moved about for much of her adult life. Returning to the United States after several overseas postings, she was tired of relocating and weary of always finding different jobs. Her résumé looked like a patchwork quilt—bush pilot, English teacher, drama coach, radio talk show host. Though interesting, none of these jobs had blossomed into a career. Now her three children were ready for college. The family required more income. Gail set her sights on a dollar amount she needed to earn. Then she framed her problem. What work would use the gifts she had, earn the money she needed, and be portable enough to go with her next time she moved overseas?

Running through many of her experiences was a common thread. She loved to learn and teach new things. That was the gift she focused on. Then, taking what could be seen as a backward step, she returned to the low-paying part-time job she had done before—teaching writing skills to business employees. But this time she set her sights higher; she was determined to break into a field that had excellent earning potential—organizational development.

She began by broadening her course offerings to include communication and team building. Then she went after free-lance contracts. Finding that she still had time on her hands, she used it for more learning herself. Rather than choosing graduate school, Gail selected the Center for Creative Leadership in Greensboro, North Carolina, for advanced training. Through colleagues she met there, she identified a young and growing consulting firm in her area that was doing what she wanted to do.

Willing at first to take jobs the senior people did not want, she gradually readied herself for more demanding contracts. Now, traveling around the country, she offers week-long training sessions to top management. Into these she pours her enthusiasm, sense of adventure, teaching skills, love of language, dramatic ability, and playful nature. Her career started with a problem to be solved and has evolved into a vocation she enjoys immensely.

If you look at Nathan's life, you see a different picture. Lovingly and expertly he is restoring a two-hundred-year-old country home for himself and his partner. Together they plan and serve gourmet meals to raise funds for a charity they especially believe in. To earn money to live, Nathan works at the local post office. That job supports his real passion, historical preservation, which he does on his own time.

Gail and Nathan have put together packages that work for them. To learn how five other people figured out how to make the money they needed by doing what they love, see appendix A. Two questions help us do this for ourselves:

- Which of my gifts cry out for expression?
- Where are these gifts needed?

In other words, what do I want to give? And what does the market need?

As the author of a book on finding what she calls "right livelihood," Marsha Sinetar has been asked in the uncertain economic climate of the early 1990s, "Can one expect to do work that one loves when it's hard enough to find any work at all?"

Her answer is revealing. Not everyone, she notes, is ready to "seek viable, fulfilling, personal vocational options."[10] It takes an emotionally mature person to practice the philosophy of right livelihood as taught by the Buddha. We become enlightened, according to this teaching, through sticking to mundane tasks, using tiresome and repetitive work to increase our mindfulness, and through meeting each moment like "gifted, focused artists."[11]

The result is self-realization, high-quality products and services, and money, but perhaps not as effortlessly or instantaneously as we would wish. Sinetar writes, "Yes, money follows right livelihood. Sorry, no one has a spreadsheet on how much or how soon. This is not the planet for such guarantees. However, it's obvious the world does chase after high-quality anything: character, goods, services, craftsmanship. The marketplace actively courts those few, rare souls who master themselves and consequently, their vocations."[12]

> **EXERCISE**
> - Add the gifts that your partner helped you name during the Gathering to the list of gifts you've already made. Now take a good look at all of them. Revel in what you have discovered. At this point, which gifts would you like to use on the job? Do some seem more alive for you than others?

Give yourself time to reflect. Then star those that seem most important to include in work now and in the future.

- Write the names of these starred gifts on the Summary Page that you've created for this chapter in your notebook (see the Introduction). As you gather clues and fragments of information about yourself in this process, you will develop clarity about yourself and what you want to offer at work. The Summary Pages will help you chart your progress visually as you move forward.

Summarize your learnings from this chapter. How do you want to act on them? What further questions do you have?

Incorporate MEANING in Work

Genuine meaning is never abstract, it is always personal. It is what moves us, stirs us, and leaves us transformed. . . . We live first; we reflect later. First, people need to articulate their own experience, then, to discern the unique pattern and unity that give their life meaning. Brita L. Gill-Austern

1 What Are You For?

Asked what she was going to do after graduation, Elsa spoke her mind: "I know where I'm going to college," she said, "but I haven't the foggiest idea what I'm going to do after that. All I know is I'd like my work to make a difference, to mean something." Elsa is not alone. Longings for worthwhile work are common and can hit us at any stage of life: starting out, mid-life, retirement.

Our desire for meaningful work compels us to look at meaning itself—first, what gives our life meaning, and then, how to incorporate that in our vocation. This, expressed in shorthand, is our second step:

Incorporate MEANING in work.

Speaking at a high school commencement, Governor Mario Cuomo of New York included these words:

> Do you think they [our children] would believe us if we told them today what we know to be true: That after the pride of obtaining a degree and, maybe later, another degree, and after their first few love affairs, that after earning their first big title, their first shiny new car, and traveling around the world for the first time and having had it all . . . they will discover that none of it counts unless they have something real and permanent to believe in.[1]

Governor Cuomo laid it on the line: without "something real and permanent to believe in," what we have and what we do has no meaning. Articulating our personal sense of meaning is one of life's major challenges.

The audience that Governor Cuomo chose for this message is significant—high school students about to make their way into the world. This is when it begins. First, a nagging feeling, then an insistent question, "What shall I do with my life?" and then, even more basic, "Why?"

Finding meaning is the process of bringing to light and describing the significance of what we value. In her book *Pathfinders*, writer Gail Sheehy concludes that the characteristic "that correlates most closely with optimum life satisfaction is the sense that 'my life has meaning.'"[2] To search for meaning is not a luxury restricted to those with a natural bent for philosophy. Rather it is what Sheehy found to be the key ingredient for a fulfilling life.

It may be that in times past a sense of meaning was easier to come by than it is now. Established authorities such as government, church, or school were trusted to offer a vision for society and a challenge to work for the common good.

Incorporate MEANING in Work

With the Iran-Contra and television evangelism scandals, that trust has eroded. More than ever, we must probe our own inner wisdom to reveal what truly matters to us.

This chapter helps you do this. First, you'll explore several sources of meaning in your own life (Segments 1-4), then you'll articulate the ideals you wish to express in your work (Segment 5), and finally you'll create specific ways to do this (Segment 7).

The sources of meaning we'll examine are vision, experience, calling, and community. Each of these can be a gold mine. Some will yield much treasure, others less. Though these are not the only sources, we've found them to be rich areas for investigation.

Vision is our starting point. If, like Elsa, you want your work to matter, what kind of future do you wish to create for yourself and those who follow you? Vision is a picture of that preferred future for which you want to work. It is a visual expression of your ideals, convictions, and those "real and permanent" beliefs referred to by Governor Cuomo.

Ask yourself, "What would our world look like if it worked right?" Answers come fairly readily:

"People would give each other a fair deal."

"We would respect diversity of cultures."

"Everyone would have housing."

"Products would be made with excellent craftsmanship."

"Kids' creativity would be cultivated."

But go deeper and ask, "Which of the visions that come to mind do I truly care about, do I long for from my depths? Which do I feel passionate about? Which will I work for?"

Andrea, a young corporate lawyer on Wall Street, was bored. She had come to think of her work as merely "making rich people richer." On a break, she set out for her favorite beach. Ever since she could remember, her summer vacations had been spent at this particular spot on the Jersey shore. Picture her there on a sunny July day two years ago. Already in her bathing suit, she hops out of the car. With towel in hand, she runs toward the waves, only to be stopped dead in her tracks by a sign posted rudely in the sand:

CLOSED
Water unsafe for swimming

The reality of what that sign meant disgusted her. How could this happen to the beautiful place she had enjoyed each year since childhood? Her memory flashed back to endless days swimming in the clear ocean waters, or marvelling at the teeming life that inhabited the tidal pools.

Now this lovely stretch of New Jersey coast was closed. Hospital waste, including used syringes, had been found washed ashore. It was a crime. Andrea could feel the anger tighten in her throat.

Outraged, she knew she wanted to do something, but what? She wondered whether there might be a way to use her legal experience for some sort of environmental work, perhaps as an advocate for clean water. Years of appreciating shore life had shown Andrea the fragility and interconnectedness of various plants and animals. She was convinced this delicate balance must be preserved. This was a vision she could work for.

To see her sacred spot threatened ignited Andrea's passion. This spurred her to action. The next day she started a job search in environmental law. Vision, fueled by passion, is a common source of meaning. Passion, whether caused by profound discontent or fierce hope, moves us from the armchair into the street.

Oddly enough, having a heartfelt vision and lacking one go hand in hand. It is not uncommon to recognize, "I don't have a vision." Is this because your ability to dream was damaged by those who did not see the value of the hopes you held? Is it that your imagination cannot picture workable alternatives to situations you consider hurtful or unproductive? Or is it that you have given up on the possibility that there is a solution?

In her workshops, Buddhist scholar Joanna Macy helps people regain a sense of vision about the future. She encourages them to look at social problems honestly and to name and share their feelings of apathy or discouragement. This releases energy for envisioning how a healthy planet would function and how they could contribute to this vision. She encourages us not to hide them but to name them, feel them, share them, and in that community of sharing to envision alternatives and then work for them. When the starkness of despair is not faced, apathy, numbness, and isolationism take hold and cause a general malaise in the culture and in individuals.[3]

No one wants to add to such a malaise. It's much more fun and productive to commit our lives and work to realizing the truth of this gospel song adapted by Bruce Thomas:

> Soon and very soon
> We're going to change the world.
> Soon and very soon
> We're going to change the world.

Soon and very soon
We're going to change the world.
For ever, ever,
we're going to change the world.[4]

With that as our stance, we can get specific, asking, "How will I change the world? What contribution is mine to make?"

> **EXERCISE**
>
> Assailed by daily headlines screaming about what's wrong with the world, it is easy to identify what you oppose. You know you feel sick about endless civil strife that keeps people from reaching food supplies, banks that are no longer trustworthy, automobiles that guzzle gas.
>
> But what are you *for*? What if, like Martin Luther King, Jr., you were given your moment at the Lincoln Memorial to speak to your sisters and brothers about your dream for a better world? What would you say? More profoundly, where do you want to place your energy, your resources, your life?
>
> Create a short, imaginary speech that begins, "I have a dream . . ." In this form (or another that better suits you), write a description of the kind of world (or nation, neighborhood, family, etc.) you want to help build.
>
> What could you do *now* to begin that building process? Which of your gifts would you want to put in service of that dream?

2 The Best Teacher

Personal firsthand experience grounds our vision in what we have seen and known. "This I know to be true, because I have experienced it," we say with conviction. Our first experiences with family and home are formative. These are followed by what happens in neighborhood and school. Gradually our perspective widens. Work, relationships, travel, and organizational commitments shape us further.

Experience influences the way we see the world and our place in it. Our task now is to identify nuggets of meaning discovered through influential experiences, then to determine which ones we want to carry forward and which we want to leave behind.

Memorable experiences occur in every realm of life. Six areas to examine are: family, education, philosophy and faith, work, social context, and pain.

Some early experiences seed our sense of meaning. Others we respect although we take a different approach. And some are not valid for us.

Family. "Ours was a do-it-yourself family. We raised our own food and did most repairs ourselves," said Sandy, who was brought up in a small Tennessee farming community. Now he lives and works in a large city.

"My parents always said, 'God helps those who help themselves.' It has been their example that has made me value independence and self-reliance so much. I'm sure that's why I wanted to go into business for myself. Dad hoped I'd take over the farm. But I knew that truck farming was not for me—I wanted to get away from that."

Education. As a student, Ana majored in Spanish and spent time in Honduras polishing her language skills. There she fell in love with a Honduran man whom she later married. Living as a resident in that country for several years, Ana gained deep respect for its culture and people, as well as a growing sense that people the world over have more in common than they realize. This way of looking at humanity—as one people—has informed and reinforced Ana's drive to reach across boundaries.

Now back in the United States, Ana is dedicated to communicating her love and knowledge of Latin American culture to the students in her Spanish classes. Firsthand, long-term exposure to another culture fueled her commitment to cross-cultural education.

Philosophy and faith. Exposure to accumulated sacred wisdom feeds our sense of meaning. Scholar Matthew Fox has searched for truth in many traditions and organized his findings into what he calls the four paths of a journey of the heart:

- The heart of exaltation, awe, wonder, and delight (the positive path)
- The heart of silence, letting go, suffering, sorrow, and grieving (the negative path)
- The heart of creativity, generativity, empowerment (the creative path)

- The heart of compassion, justice-making, healing, and celebration (the transformative path)[5]

These four paths form the inner core of Matthew Fox's philosophy and outlook on life. As we sift through our own exposure to philosophy and faith, like Fox, we can identify the wisdom we wish to incorporate in our life and work.

Work. Astronaut Russell Schweickart's work took him many miles above the planet. During his walk outside an orbiting spacecraft, he truly felt the mystery of the universe. His conception of what mattered was powerfully expanded: "When you go around earth in an hour and a half, you begin to recognize that your identity is with that whole thing, and that makes a change . . . from where you see it, the thing is whole and it's so beautiful. You wish you could take one person in each hand, one from each side in various conflicts, and say, 'Look. Look at it from this perspective. Look at it! What's important?'"[6]

Few of us have the chance, as Schweickart did, to break free of terrestrial bonds so dramatically, but many of us through our work gain perspectives that broaden our horizons and deepen our understanding.

Social context. Societal influences provide elements of meaning that we may wish to express in work. Hal reminisces about the small town in central Idaho where he was raised: "We were all neighbors. Even if I didn't know someone, I knew they were friends of someone I did know. I was raised to think of the world as populated by neighbors—some close, some far, but all neighbors. For me, the man who ran the grocery exemplified this feeling. He knew everybody."

Today, years later, in a major eastern city, Hal still sees the world the same way and still lives the solid ethic it implies: neighborliness. At first it was hard for him—the big city seemed to laugh at his naïveté. However, after he took a job as a Safeway checker, things began to fall into place for Hal. Here's how he describes it: "I know my job seems boring to some people, but I really love being part of people's everyday life. Shopping is such a drag for most folks; I like to pick up their spirits, make small talk about their families and all, create that sense of neighborliness I knew as a kid."

Pain and grief. Depending on how we respond to it, adversity also contains clues to meaning. Brendan, stricken with cancer, came to know with new clarity what he had only vaguely felt all his life—that life is a precious gift from God. Life is short; each moment is a treasure. This insight shaped the last work he was to do in his life.

Noticing that his doctors were uncomfortable talking with him about what it really felt like to be ill, he decided to help physicians relate to their dying patients with increased warmth and understanding. Inviting each doctor on the ward to spend some time with him, listening to his experience, he offered suggestions about the kind of personal sharing he thought other patients would appreciate.

EXERCISE

List several influential life experiences you want to explore for insights into what holds meaning for you now. Consider the areas already mentioned or others of your choosing. For each item list two or three messages that came to you through these experiences. Circle the ones you want to carry forward in your life.

Here is what Sandy listed and circled under Family and then under Faith and Philosophy:

FAMILY

- our family is meant to till this land
- (be responsible and self-reliant)
- fix things; don't buy new ones when old ones work
- (work hard!)

FAITH and PHILOSOPHY

- (the world was created by a loving spirit)
- my religion has <u>the</u> answers
- (life contains both light and darkness)
- people should take care of themselves

Incorporate MEANING in Work

Do this same process with each area you choose. Now on a separate sheet of paper make a meaning collage showing key messages you want to carry forward from each source you explored. Create the collage from the circled items. The following example shows the collage Sandy began to make.

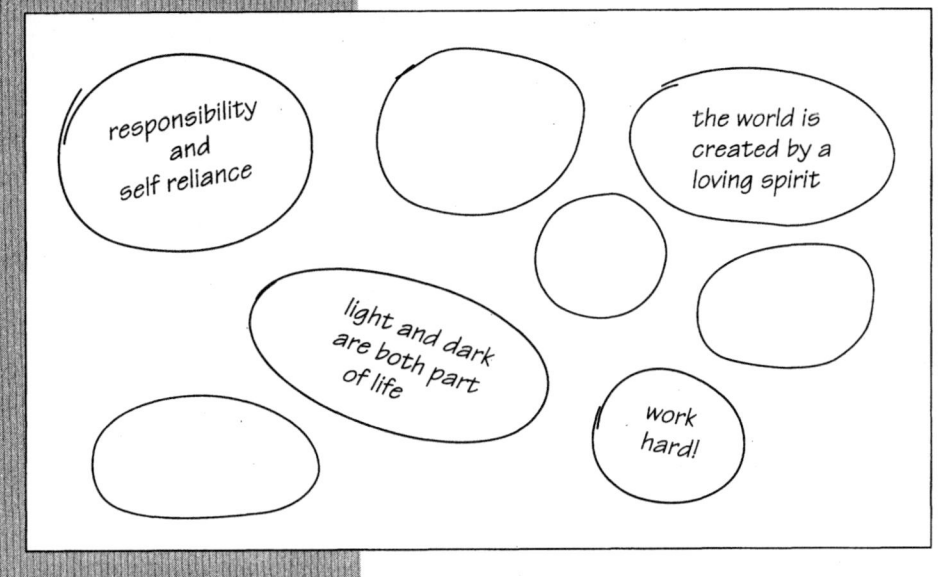

3 Calling—A Whisper or a Yell

In the 1970s, writer Studs Terkel crisscrossed the country for his book *Working*, interviewing people about "what they do all day and how they feel about what they do." From hundreds of quotations, he selected the words of Nora Watson as the most succinct expression of people's yearnings: "I think most of us are looking for a calling, not a job. Most of us, like the assembly line worker, have jobs that are too small for our spirit. Jobs are not big enough for people."[7]

The Latin word for "to call" is *vocare*. This is the root for our word *vocation*, that inner summons that makes us feel there is something we are meant to do through our work. A sense of calling is a powerful source of meaning.

A calling is powerful because it will not let us go. Futurist Marilyn Ferguson describes this power in her own words and those of psychiatrist C. G. Jung:

> Speaking of his own experience, Jung said, "Vocation acts like a law of God from which there is no escape." The creative person is overpowered, captive of and driven by a demon. Unless one assents to the power of the inner voice, the personality cannot evolve. Although we often mistreat those who listen to that voice, he said, still "they become our legendary heroes."[8]

People experience vocation in at least two ways: as something *given and received* or as something *constructed and cultivated*.

We know people who have been given and who have received a calling. Perhaps we envy them. Who or what calls them? The inner voice may be a *strong gift* crying to be used. "I've built things ever since I can remember. I knew I wanted construction to be part of my work." It may be the voice of a *particular profession or craft* that has been hallowed in our experience and seems especially suited to our ideals and gifts. "We come from a long line of doctors. It never occurred to me to be anything but a doctor." *Circumstances* call. When Meirad Corrigan watched the murder of her nephew at the hands of Irish terrorists, she then and there vowed to work for peace in Ireland. An *empowering vision* summons people to work for it. Huge numbers of people, for example, now feel called by the deterioration of our environment to vocations that deal with the damage. People of faith experience call as a feeling of being addressed by *God or the message of their faith*.

If you are a person who has been called in this way, the task is to listen to the voices that are calling and obey the summons.

However, you may not hear any voices. You may be like Dan, an idealistic man in his thirties, who said, "I'd love to be knocked off my horse by a thunderbolt containing a message 'Do this!' Then I would gladly obey." Or you may be like Meg, an executive secretary who exclaimed, "I'd like to hear a call, but all I hear is a whisper!" You might not even hear that. Perhaps you experience only the static of confusion; that is not unusual.

Many people have a hard time discovering a sense of vocation. No predominant talent, personality trait, or interest insists on expression. For these people, a sense of calling comes as the result of painstakingly constructing a deeply motivating view of their work. This describes Dan, who says: "It dawned on me that I have many selves that need feeding through work. There is the self I call Village Elder. He wants to be at the center of local government, making things work for a community. But pulling in another direction is Wanderlust—the guy who wants to see the world, be on the go. Then there is Writer, who'd love to craft a beautiful piece of unforgettable prose."

What liberated Dan was naming these parts of himself. He then began to think about which type of work each self wanted. Finally, another breakthrough occurred. "I realized that one lifelong career wouldn't do it for me. I had to let go of that. To realize that no one career would have to be forever made me much more imaginative."

Dan began to ask, "Which part of myself is ready to lead now career-wise?" Village Elder won the vote and led him to a position as an assistant to the mayor of a neighboring city. When his boss lost the next election, Dan was out of a job. Gradually Wanderlust got the upper hand. Overseas positions were all Dan considered. Now, in Latvia, he helps the Peace Corps train volunteers to work with small businesses.

Asked how all this connects to a sense of calling, Dan replies, "No calling has ever jumped out at me, much as I wish it would. But what I am beginning to see is a common thread in all the things I'd like to do. This seems more an inkling than a calling, but I see that over and over I choose work that involves me in 'empowering people.' However overused the term, that's what kept me in local government and took me overseas."

In a sense, those who hear a call, and even Dan, who thought about his different vocational selves, have some sense of clarity about what they want to do. You may not yet have this sort of clarity but still know you want the same sense of focus and purpose. The experience of C. G. Jung may offer some help and encouragement. At a midpoint in his life, Jung felt confused about his life's direction: "After the parting of the ways with Freud, a period of inner uncertainty began for me. It would be no exaggeration to call it a state of disorientation. I felt totally suspended in mid-air, for I had not yet found my footing."[9]

To give outward expression to this inner confusion, each morning Jung created "a small circular drawing, a mandala, which seemed to correspond to my inner situation at the time." Each day he allowed images to emerge from deep within. These he expressed in color and form. Questioning whether there was a goal for this process, he came to conclude that he had to "let myself be carried along by the current, without a notion of where it would lead me."[10]

Only later did he realize that the goal he was unconsciously pursuing was to be centered in his own being, to find his point of view as differentiated from that of his mentor, Sigmund Freud. From then on, a new sense of calling emerged. He began more original investigations into how the psyche works and incorporated these new insights into his work with patients.

You may wish to allow images from within yourself to guide you to your sense of calling. As Jung did, invite them to emerge. Listen to what they say. Go with your gut! It has wisdom for you.

EXERCISE

The voices that call people to vocation were identified in this segment as

- A strong gift crying to be used
- A particular profession or craft especially suited to our ideals or gifts
- Circumstances that compel our response
- An empowering vision
- God or the message of faith

Add other voices to this list if they occur to you. Record your reflections on call. Here are three ways to gain content for these reflections.

1. Take the above list with you on a meditative walk. Are any of these voices present in your life? How are they calling to you? What are they saying? Record in writing what you wish to remember.
2. Read over Dan's experience. What insights do you gain related to your own sense of calling? Record them in writing.
3. If C. G. Jung's experience as just described rings a bell with you, consider creating a mandala.

   Draw a circle on a piece of paper—perhaps a foot in diameter. Using color and form, depict your call to meaningful work. Include images, colors, symbols, lines, and forms that occur spontaneously. Don't try to make something happen or draw a clear picture of anything. Let your unconscious guide you. In other words, just see what happens. Over a period of days, consider drawing several mandalas.

   Use a few minutes to look at what you've drawn. Then write down what occurs to you as you look at it. Or do some journal writing about what you drew. What are these mandalas telling you about your own calling to meaningful work?

4 Community as a Source of Meaning

At twenty-nine, Katherine was one of the youngest to become a principal in the consulting firm where she worked. But something was missing. Well qualified for her personnel management position by an excellent graduate record at a leading management school, she was on the fast track. Considered successful according to outward standards, she felt inwardly depleted. Her achievements became less and less meaningful to her. Yet she had no time to figure out why this was so.

Suddenly, illness stopped her in her tracks. Never having taken much time for friendship, she was surprised when neighbors and colleagues offered help. "The ways in which people popped up to give support were miraculous to me," she exclaimed. This touched her deeply and filled some of the emptiness she had felt.

She recognized that she had been operating in such a self-sufficient manner that it was only illness that could open her to the friendship others wanted to offer.

This was her first experience of community. It made her want to build more of it into her life. Starting with family, which had been distant, she tried to help them "feel more closeness and love." After occasional attendance at church, she decided to become a member so she could feel "a community there." Deciding to participate in one of our seminars, she said, "I crave the small experiences and sharing that I shunned while working because they wasted time that could be billed by the hour."

Sociologist Robert Bellah and his team, in their book *Habits of the Heart*, identify community as a primary source of meaning in people's lives. Their description of community is illuminating:

> *Community* is a term used very loosely by Americans today. We use it in a strong sense: a *community* is a group of people who are socially interdependent, who participate together in discussion and decision making, and who share certain *practices* . . . that both define the community and are nurtured by it. Such a community is not quickly formed. It almost always has a history and so is also a *community of memory*, defined in part by its past and its memory of its past.[11]

Bellah and his associates note many such communities in the United States: ethnic, racial, religious, geographical, and national. We know these communities and may have participated in some of them—the Sons of Italy, the Black Caucus, St. Mary's Church on the corner, the farm community on Rural Route 1, the people of this nation.

Genuine communities provide building blocks that help us construct systems of meaning that have staying power. Communities have a *history* and thus root us in the past. They posit a *future* on which to base hope. *Heroes and heroines* embody and exemplify what has meaning for the community and model for us the meaningful life. According to Bellah and his team, *stories* "that make up a tradition contain conceptions . . . of what a good person is like." There are stories, as well, about how suffering has been faced. Thus communities put forward pictures of what makes for *success* and also of what constitutes loving *support*. Communities participate in what Bellah calls *practices of commitment*, those acts that keep the community alive. They evolve a *language* through which to express what matters most to them.[12]

We don't have to "reinvent the wheel" in order to find meaning. By actively participating in communities that embody our values, we build on the wisdom of those who have gone before us—providing we choose and create communities that share the values and convictions we want to embody ourselves and not those that have been thrust upon us.

Yet no community is perfect. When you look for gold, you find the genuine article and also slag—minerals that have no value. Even the best of communities have their share of both. It's worth sorting through the slag to find the valuable stuff.

EXERCISE

Here's a quick and revealing way to mine the communities you're part of for nuggets of meaning that have staying power for you. You will need:

- A glass of lemonade
- Two pieces of paper
- A pen or pencil
- Fifteen minutes of time alone

Begin by sitting down and taking a few deep breaths and two sips of lemonade. Relax! On one piece of paper, create a symbol for each community in which you participate: for example, your colleagues at work, a neighborhood organization, a church.

Place this "community poster" where you can see it easily. Remember that in these communities are people who share your values and are

> working for the same things you are. They are your cheering section and your "meaning professors." In your mind, ask each of them, "What bits of meaning do you offer that touch me deeply?" Write these on the poster.
>
> Now take a couple more deep breaths and another sip of lemonade. On the top of your other paper write, "These Make My Life Worth Living." Then begin writing. Don't think too hard or try to sound deep and philosophical. Just let it come off the top. Simply answer the question, "What is it that makes my life worth the ride?"
>
> When you finish, put your papers where you can see them easily. Maybe on your nightstand, the refrigerator, or the bathroom mirror—someplace visible. Let them be a reminder of your connections to life . . . the connections that make life more than existence.[13]

5 Collect Your Ideals

So far in this chapter, you've been in an exploring mode, collecting pieces of meaning from a consideration of vision, experience, vocation, and community. Look at what you have collected, see how each piece relates to the others, and then select and combine those you wish most to express through work. In other words, distill the essence!

Let's take a look at how Stan, a musician in his late thirties, has done this. In writing, he described key points in his life and "meaning lessons" learned.[14] Stan's high school years were spent in Taiwan. There he was assailed by stark contrast. Grinding poverty existed alongside magnificent mansions whose opulence was just visible behind formidable walls.

At Taipei American School, Stan remembers: "I had teachers who influenced me deeply . . . who wanted to teach. These folks loved life, and, as teachers, amazed me at being interested in what I thought! I found myself talking at length about many topics that I never knew I had feelings about. It was at this time that I recall developing faith that people could have ideals: *love was possible in this dangerous, jaded, hurtful world.*"

Recalling even earlier experiences at elementary school, he remembered, "This was a time I affirmed several things. *I love to read. I love to create. I love to craft things with care.*"

After graduation, when Stan's buddies went off to college, his folks returned to the United States. Stan chose to remain in Taiwan and go to work. Without family and friends, he was lonely. "While it went against my grain, I begrudgingly began to accept that this pain and loneliness I felt was in some way OK, 'character building.' I began to write music—string quartets, various combinations for trios and duets as musicians were available. This became my main source of joy. *In a world where I could not count on a set of beliefs or other people to ease my deep sense of isolation and alienation, music was a form of self-renewal."*

Skipping to the present, this is how Stan describes the cultural climate today:

> We live in a special time. Society is rapidly changing. Men and women are redefining relationships thousands of years old. Women are demanding equality, and men who can't handle it are losing out. Men who can't handle it are confused, hurt, out of work, and often unable to find much happiness—the society no longer validates sexist points of view. Similarly, this decade is a time of international tensions and major shifts in powers that once defined global relationships.
>
> *It is a time for the Chinese [language] character for crisis, symbolizing two different things: danger and opportunity.*

Reflecting on his own sense of vocation at this point, Stan says that he feels moved to offer his musical gifts for "healing men and women, East and West, North and South." Specifically, this means sharing a vision with his music to offer "sustenance for the soul," to offer "a message of hope," and to help people find from a story or song new courage to carry on.

This is the *meaning stew* Stan concocted from collecting the ideals he wants to express through work.

Native American storyteller Jose Hobday recalls that her parents did something similar for her when she was born into her Seneca tribe. Gathering objects representing sources of power, they placed them in a special medicine bag, which was later presented to her. Included were earth from the place where she was born, a pulverized piece of the umbilical cord, and a secret contribution from her father that symbolized the spiritual sustenance that he hoped for for his child.[15]

Through the years this bag has reminded Jose of special insights that come to her through her people. Its ingredients put her in touch with the *medicine* or truth she uniquely has to contribute.

Incorporate MEANING in Work

> **EXERCISE**
>
> Look over the work you have done thus far in this chapter—your statement of vision, the meaning mosaic you made from influential experiences, your reflections on call, the messages you carry forward from communities you have known.
>
> Then, like Stan, summarize the meaning you wish to express through your work. Put this in writing and call it your meaning statement. Symbols can serve to reinforce what you want to remember. Thus you might also like to
>
> - create a medicine bag with objects that symbolize what you expressed in your meaning statement, or
> - create another expression of your own.

6 Gathering

Purpose: To gain further clarity on the meaning and vision you want to incorporate in work

Leaders Bring: Newsprint, masking tape, marking pencils, 10-foot length of string or yarn, 3 x 5 cards

Everyone Bring: Meaning mosaic from Segment 2, reflections on call from Segment 3, and meaning statement from Segment 5

WARM-UP (EVERYONE)
15 MINUTES

Taking turns, stand up and assume the character of one of your influential family members.

1. Introduce your character.
2. With your character's voice, describe some of the values that character wants to pass on to you.

3. Now, returning to your own identity, describe how these values influenced you—what you retained, discarded, or modified.

SUPPORT AND FEEDBACK (IN THREES)
30 MINUTES

1. Review your reflections on call from Segment 3.
2. Each person shares what they wish about their sense of call—feelings, insights, questions.
3. Allow time for listeners to ask questions and express support. Give each person about eight minutes to share and receive feedback.

ENCOURAGEMENT AND AFFIRMATION (EVERYONE)
30 MINUTES

1. Give each member a 3 x 5 card. (Partners take several.)
2. Use string to form a small circle (about three feet across) on the floor or table. This is the wish pool. Sit around it.
3. Each member: Read your meaning mosaic (from Segment 2) to yourself. Based on that, write a wish for the world on your card. Place your name on the card. (Partners write two or three wishes on separate cards.) Place the cards in the wish pool.
4. Spend several minutes silently reflecting on your wish.
5. Slowly, as the mood moves you, read out loud your meaning statement. Allow time for each one to speak. When everyone has finished, each person dips into the wish pool, taking a card someone else has written (partners each take half the cards), and then in a celebrating voice pronounces, "I wish for . . . (whatever is written on the card.)"

COMPLETION (EVERYONE)
10 MINUTES

Spend time discussing your feelings and insights about the activities you did in this Gathering.

CLOSING (EVERYONE)
5 MINUTES

Refer back to page 31 for suggestions for closing.

7 Create and Embody Your Best Work

Organization consultant Peter Block believes that each of us is the prime architect of our work. In his book *The Empowered Manager* he encourages us to create a vision of greatness for our work and to choose specific ways to embody it daily.[16] It is not unusual, Block points out, for organizations to forge vision statements. Equally important is the task of each person, not just those at the top, to create a vision of greatness for their work. From this act of creation comes meaning.[17]

People balk when Block urges them to go for greatness. Is it not too flamboyant, arrogant, or presumptuous? No, he argues, it spurs us to dream extravagantly, and that motivates us to act. "Greatness demands that we eliminate caution, that we eliminate our reservations, and that we have hope in the face of the history of our limitations," he writes.[18] By definition, your vision for greatness will be impractical and make you feel you're shooting for the stars.

When you visualize the most enticing picture of work you can imagine, you can work to create that each day by your every act. Most of us underestimate our personal ability to effect change no matter how high or low we are on the ladder of achievement. As Block reminds us,

> Lasting improvement does not take place by pronouncements or official programs. Change takes place slowly inside each of us and by the choices we think through in quiet wakeful moments lying in bed just before dawn. Culture is changed not so much by carefully planned, dramatic, and visible events as by focusing on our own actions in the small, barely noticed, day-to-day activities of our work.[19]

Early in this century, the Christman Brothers from New York City created a vision of greatness for the pianos they manufactured. They committed themselves to producing the most beautiful tone and most responsive action possible in their keyboard instruments. Company craftsmen were encouraged to select the finest wood, to fashion it meticulously into beautiful parts, and to assemble each piano with great precision. Every blotter, ruler, and other advertising piece pictured the Christman Brothers handsome studio grand piano, top opened, ready to reveal its superb quality. Under the picture was the motto "The First Touch Tells." That logo and motto epitomized all the commitment to fine craftsmanship and customer service that the Christman Piano Company stood for.

These piano makers exemplified what Peter Block encourages each of us to do—to contemplate the meaning we want to express in work and then to live it each day in the hundreds of choices we make.

EXERCISE

Create a vision of greatness for your own work (what you do now or what you wish to do). Write down at least three ways you want to express this at work or in your search for work. Be specific and concrete. Devise a way to bring this about.

Then, for fun, create a logo and a motto that depicts the particular meaning you wish most to convey through your work. Enter this on your Meaning Summary Page along with anything else you want to remember.

Summarize the things you have learned from this chapter. How do you want to act on them? What further questions do you have?

Determine How PARAMETERS Shape Choices

Meaningful work is important; so is a decent salary. Finding ways to bridge those frequently divergent paths may be one of the key quests of our generation. Norman Boucher and Laura Tennen

1 How Parameters Influence Choice

So far, you've focused on hopes and dreams. However, untethered balloons are soon lost from sight and become but a memory. In addition to looking at the gifts you wish to use and the meaning you want to express in work, you also need to relate your aspirations to reality. Don't groan! Reality can be refreshing. Your vocational choices are influenced not only by what you love to do but also by what you *must* do to live the way you want to or need to at this time. Practical parameters, along with gifts and meaning, are part of the root system you bring from yourself to work. They ground you.

How those closest to you feel about what you do, your state of health, and your stage in life are factors that influence how much energy and time you have for work, the money you need to earn, and the geographical location of your work.

Limitation narrows choices. And that's not all bad. The key step of this chapter focuses on the impact of your life situation on work choices.

Determine how PARAMETERS shape choices.

Simple to state but tough to do—because there are lots of ways to deal with the reality of your situation.

Consider health. You might feel that nothing is so limiting as a physical disability. But look at Ted Kennedy, Jr. Losing his leg to cancer motivated him to help others adjust to similar circumstances. A missing leg is a fixed condition, yes. But how that influences your work is as flexible as you allow yourself to be.

Consider money. You own a house and support a family. That requires a certain amount of money. You might see that amount as given. But is it? Your kids and your spouse might find it exciting to sell all the family's worldly possessions and join you in one of the developing nations.

The work of this chapter invites you to see how parameters have shaped your past choices (Segment 1); identify your present parameters (Segment 2); take action to change parameters you wish to change (Segment 3); deal with obstacles blocking you (Segment 4); make peace with parameters you cannot change (Segment 5); and allow those parameters you cannot change to help shape your choices (Segment 7).

Practical parameters do influence work choices, but the form of that influence varies. Some parameters you must accept. That may feel like a limitation — and so it is — but a limit is not only a restriction. A limitation is also a priority that you choose to honor. For example, if you say, "I can't do that because of my family," you may feel restricted by your situation. The flip side of that limitation is positive, however: "My family is a priority for me." Celebrate the integrity of your choice.

Some of your parameters you may wish to change. To find more time to care for little children you might change your work hours. To make more money, you might market your skills differently.

By limiting choice, parameters help focus decision making. In this age of too many choices, it can be a relief to know that some parameters cannot change. "My spouse's job requires frequent moves. If I want to live with him, my work will have to be portable." That insight narrowed Beth's choices and helped her decide to use her marketing skills to become a children's clothing buyer. That way, she could work anywhere in the country.

By the same token, lack of parameters can be disconcerting. "With Maria no longer here and my children not in the area, I can do pretty much what I want to do in retirement," says Bill. "But don't feel happy for me. I wish I had some constraints that would limit my choices a bit. Total freedom is really scary." With no real limitations, Bill must rely on preference alone to guide his choices about what to do, where to live, and what satisfactions a job should deliver.

The realities of our lives, even when difficult, can be great energizers. Newly divorced with three young children to raise, Nancy was at first overwhelmed. "I have to support the kids all by myself," she said. "How am I going to do that?" Nancy took a step at a time, gradually determining what she needed to earn, where she would live, and the kind of work she would like to do. Resolving these issues increased her confidence and gave her courage to begin serious job hunting. Today she is successful because she took charge of her life step by step.

EXERCISE

To get a feel for how parameters have influenced your own vocational decisions, think back to the past. List four or five experiences in which practical parameters shaped work choices you made.

2 Sort and Sift

Our society no longer has fixed roles for men and women regarding work. Each person must sort and sift priorities and parameters. Columnist Ellen Goodman describes the kinds of choices we are up against:

> Carol chose. She wanted the promotion so much she could taste it. But the job came with weekends and evenings and traveling attached, and she didn't want to miss that time with her husband and sons. She couldn't do both. Knowing that didn't make it any easier.
>
> Carol isn't the only one I know making these decisions. Another friend refused to move up a rung on the professional ladder because it would have meant uprooting his family and transferring his wife out of a career of her own. A third couple consciously put their careers on the back burner in order to spend time with the family they'd merged out of two previous marriages.
>
> ... The decisions they faced are the rock-bottom ones, the toughies. How do you divide the pie of your life—your own time and energy?[1]

When you reflect on the parameters of your life, you may find more options than you thought were available for dealing with them. You may even discover that the parameters you consider limiting are a source of energy and direction.

EXERCISE

The following Practical Parameters Inventory considers the limits of your life—time, money, location, relationships, health, and age. The purpose of the Inventory is to help you identify your present parameters and decide which are firm, which you want to change, and how they shape work choices.

PRACTICAL PARAMETERS INVENTORY

Directions: You can use the inventory to gain clarity on present or future work choices. Decide which you want to focus on now. Check your preferences in each section. If your preference is not described adequately, describe the option that works best for you. Then write in your notebook or on cards answers to the Sum-

Determine How PARAMETERS Shape Choices 59

mary and Reaction questions at the end of each section. If you, like Bill, lack practical parameters, go through the inventory and note your preferences under each category.

TIME

Time is a primary consideration in thinking about your desired work situation and how it balances with other parts of your life. As you think about the future, what are your time requirements?

How much time do I need or want to work?

- ☐ Full-time with limited overtime
- ☐ Full-time
- ☐ Part-time
- ☐ Other: _____

What kind of work hours do I want to keep?

- ☐ Regular daytime hours — occasional overtime
- ☐ Regular daytime hours — no overtime
- ☐ Rotating schedule
- ☐ Nighttime
- ☐ Flextime
- ☐ I want control of work hours
- ☐ Other: _____

How much time do I want to budget for nonwork activities?

- ☐ Specific time for myself each week: _____
- ☐ Time for relationships: _____
- ☐ Time for other activities (list activities): _____

_____
_____
_____

Summary and Reaction

(The following questions are the same for all parameters to be examined.)

- **What time parameters must my work have?**
  (Summarize in writing the items you checked above. For example, "My work must be full-time, weekday evenings, allowing several hours daily with my family.")
- **How do I feel about this?**
  (Record your feelings as accurately as you can. They will fuel your answers to the next question. Know that feelings change. If you take this inventory another time, your feelings could be quite different.)
- **How will I respond to this reality?**
  (Note whether you want to change the parameter or your attitude toward it, or whether you accept things the way they are.)

REWARDS

In addition to "putting bread on the table," rewards also include levels of responsibility, recognition, personal satisfaction, and the impact you have on other people and situations.

What role does my income play in meeting the financial needs of my household?

- ☐ I am the sole earner in my household.
- ☐ I am the major earner in the household.
- ☐ I am a co-earner and need to share expenses.
- ☐ I am a secondary earner and must contribute a percentage of expenses.

What are my financial needs?

- ☐ Above $80,000
- ☐ Above $60,000
- ☐ Above $30,000
- ☐ $20,000–$30,000
- ☐ Below $20,000

Determine How PARAMETERS Shape Choices

☐ Money is not a primary consideration. I will go forward with my vocational choice regardless of what I earn.
☐ Other: _____

How important are benefits (vacation, insurance, etc.)?

☐ Major consideration
☐ Secondary consideration
☐ Not important
☐ Other: _____

How much responsibility do I want?

☐ Major responsibility
☐ Medium responsibility
☐ Minimal responsibility
☐ Act as supervisor
☐ Be closely supervised
☐ Have minimal supervision
☐ Other: _____

How much recognition do I require from others for what I do?

☐ Substantial
☐ Some
☐ None
☐ Other: _____

How much personal satisfaction do I need from a job?

☐ I must love what I do.
☐ I must like what I do
☐ Other: _____

How much impact do I want to have?

☐ My work must affect many people and/or situations.
☐ My work must affect some people and/or situations.

- ☐ My work must affect a few people and/or situations.
- ☐ My work must affect someone.
- ☐ Other: _____

Summary and Reaction
- ■ What rewards should my work provide?
- ■ How do I feel about this?
- ■ How will I respond to this reality?

LOCATION

How do geographic considerations affect your decision making?

Is the geographic location of my work a limiting factor?
- ☐ My work must be in my present location.
- ☐ My work must be in my present location for now, but later on it can be someplace else.
- ☐ My work can be in any of the following locations:

  _____
  _____
  _____

- ☐ I am willing to travel.
- ☐ Other: _____

How much of a commute can I tolerate?
- ☐ Thirty to sixty minutes.
- ☐ Under thirty minutes.
- ☐ I want to be able to walk to work.
- ☐ I want to work at home.
- ☐ Other: _____

Summary and Reaction
- What location features should my work include?
- How do I feel about this?
- How will I respond to this reality?

HEALTH, LIFE STAGE, AND AGE

Factors related to the health, life stage, and age of yourself and those for whom you are responsible can limit vocational choices.

The situation for me at present is as follows:
- ☐ My choices about the time, rewards, and location of my future work are not limited by the health, life stage, or age of myself or my family
- ☐ Periodic but temporary health requirements limit my choices about the time, rewards, and location of my work (e.g., occasional medical treatment requiring hospitalization or travel)
- ☐ Health/life stage factors in myself or another family member significantly limit my choices about the time, rewards, and location of work
- ☐ Other: _____

Summary and Reaction
- How do health, life stage, and/or age factors limit the timing, reward, or location of my work?
- How do I feel about this?
- How will I respond to this reality?

PRIMARY RELATIONSHIPS

How people close to you (spouse, partner, children, housemates, friends) feel about your work can be an important consideration in what you decide to do. These people are part of the givens of your life. You may want to take into consideration their wishes. For example, Sam, an

English professor at a midwestern university, agrees to be available for calls from his daughter's school since his wife, Polly, a corporate vice-president for a large advertising firm, is often busy with clients and travels frequently.

What practical dimensions of work are important to those close to me?

- ☐ Forty-hour work week with limited overtime
- ☐ Forty-hour work week with no overtime
- ☐ No weekend work
- ☐ Limited travel
- ☐ Availability for emergency child responsibility
- ☐ Salary level
- ☐ Benefits
- ☐ Other: _____

Summary and Reaction

- ■ What practical dimensions of work do those close to me want me to consider?
- ■ How do I feel about this?
- ■ How will I respond to this reality?

3 Bust Loose

If you feel like something's got to give, chances are the time is ripe for change. Before her children arrived, Karen worked as a fashion merchandiser in a department store. She loved it. Hours were long, but she didn't care. She was in her element.

When her first child was born, conflict tore her apart. Child care arrangements proved unsatisfactory. On the job she found herself worrying more about her baby than her customers. She knew she needed a change. Again and again she found herself thinking, "I want to stay at home with my baby."

But another reality would not let her go: "I need to earn my share of the family expenses."

What to do? She asked her husband and a couple of friends to brainstorm ideas about how she could do what she loved, earn what she needed, and also remain home with the baby.

"Work weekends and earn comp time," said one.

"How about night work—have you ever considered that?"

"Do you know that you can obtain work-at-home contracts from large corporations? Have you thought about that?"

"What about creating a home-based business?"

The suggestions flew. At first confused, Karen gradually sifted the ideas until two surfaced. "I know I want to work at home so I can be available to the baby anytime, but I don't want to work for someone else—I'd like to create my own business."

That conclusion led her to talk with others who had done the same. Enrolling in a Small Business Administration course, she learned what it takes to establish a business. "I want to do it," she exclaimed, "and I'm going to go for it!" She knew she enjoyed sales and marketing, and environmental concerns had long held her interest. When a position as regional manager for a company that markets environmentally safe products came to her attention, she grabbed it, knowing that she could control much of her schedule and use her home as her primary office.

Karen found to be true what Carolyn Jabs wrote in her article "How to Kick a Dream into Action": "Once you define your path, if you continue to take even small steps, you will eventually be standing on the threshold of your goal."[2]

EXERCISE

Look over the work you did on the Practical Parameters Inventory in Segment 2. Let the different parameters interact with one another. Select the one that you most want to change or the one most possible to change. Create a notebook page or card for this parameter, then describe the specific results you want.

Brainstorm changes you could make that would bring about this result. If you need some help, ask a friend or two to join in. Remember, brainstorming means anything goes. Be crazy, wild, think of outlandish things, easy or hard—whatever might bring about the result you want.

Now sift a bit, letting two or three feasible steps surface in your mind. Write these steps on your page or card. Resolve to take these steps as soon as possible. This would be a good time to congratulate yourself for making a start!

Repeat the process for other parameters you want to change.

One last thought on changing parameters. If there are certain parameters you dream of changing but can't see a way to do so now, create a dream box. In that box place a few of your way-out wishes that, if they came true, would place you closer to your dream job. For example:

"I wish I could earn enough money to put my kids through college."

"I would love to move to Arizona and get rid of my allergies."

"I wish I had the time to write science fiction screenplays."

Every once in a while, look in your dream box. You'll be surprised how dreams change without your doing anything about them. Either a dream will be stronger, in which case you might have more momentum to make the changes you want. Or it will not matter as much anymore, and you can throw the item away with no regrets.

Dragons You Must Slay

Saint Paul, as he struggled to make some changes in his life, made a classic statement:

> My own behavior baffles me.
>
> For I find myself not doing
>
> what I really want to do.[3]

Do you also find this to be true? Do you decide to make a change, and then find yourself avoiding action? Well, welcome to the human race. That is what many of us do. It is not unusual. There are forces within and outside that oppose change.

You mention to the boss that you'd like to switch from full- to part-time work so that you'll have more time to take care of your sick wife. Accustomed to having your full-time services, the boss puts up resistance. That's natural. But that reaction can cause you to doubt your decision.

More difficult to understand are inner forces that sabotage your best intentions. Ray wanted to direct a peace institute after retiring from the military and was willing to take a substantial pay cut to do so. "But then, I began having second thoughts. This culture equates people's worth with the amount of money they earn. I know I could live on less and am willing to do that, but all of a sudden I find myself beset with worries about losing face with my friends who are in high-paying jobs."

Elizabeth O'Connor wrote a book entitled *Our Many Selves* in which she describes the many parts of ourselves that compete for attention.[4] Like unruly people who disrupt meetings, these inner selves cry out to be heard. When we name them and listen to their needs, we gain insight into how to deal with them. When Ray did this, here is what he wrote:

> My *altruistic self* is excited by directing the institute. This self wants to say yes.
>
> My *keep-up-with-the-Joneses self* wonders how taking a pay cut will look to my upwardly mobile friends. This self needs to talk over this problem with someone who understands. Until it does, this self will keep putting up delaying tactics.

Conflicting feelings may surface not only as ambivalence or confusion but also as sabotage: forgetting to make a phone call, getting sick on the day of an interview, feeling like you'd rather stay home than go to the class for which you just signed up. Change is scary, and sometimes the price is higher than you anticipated. But life without challenge and risk kills creativity and dampens the spirit. If you take the time to listen to your feelings and to get some reinforcement from people who care for you, you will find it easier to risk making changes in your life.

EXERCISE

Take another look at the practical parameter(s) you want to change (Segment 3). Jot down any feelings you have about the steps you have listed. Put a star by those feelings that might block you in carrying your plan forward.

If inner or outer forces are blocking your efforts to change specific parameters, write briefly—or, better yet, draw a picture, an image, or a symbol in response to the questions below. What colors or shapes are evoked by them? Give your creative side a chance to muse.

> - What forces are blocking you?
> - What are their characteristics?
> - What are they saying to you? Write out their messages or depict them in image form.
> - What is underneath their message—what do they really want? Describe their needs.
>
> Be quiet for a while and reflect on what you wrote. Perhaps change your activity—go for a brief walk or do something around the house. Then write or draw in response to this question:
>
> - How can I address each need that has surfaced so that it will receive attention and not block my desire for change?

5. The Many Uses of the Fixed Parameter

Let's face it. Not all parameters can be changed. Consider Harry, for example: "Everyone said that I had it made when I married Natasha. She's got a great job pulling down big money in some hot-shot law firm downtown. But to tell you the truth, it's put a crimp in my wanderlust. We're stuck in Seattle."

OK, Harry's not going anywhere. But he's made peace with that "fixed" portion of his life. "I love Tasha. I want to be with her, and I want the best for her. So over time I've taken that old restlessness and channeled it into other pursuits. I've been counseling runaways. You know I can feel where they're coming from."

Segment 1 introduced the idea that fixed parameters, freely chosen, point to another priority that is being supported. Hank and Joy are a two-career couple. "Equality of job opportunity is of central concern in our relationship," says Joy. Hank echoes her thought. "We try to take turns following each other's job choices," Joy explains. "When I was offered a position in Boston, Hank transferred. Then it was his turn. When his career dictated that we move to Akron, I gritted my teeth and found new work there." For Hank and Joy, equality is a value sufficiently strong to dictate where they will work.

Parameters that seem fixed can also help you decide on certain kinds of work. They give you information about job choice that must be weighed in with other factors. After Louise finished graduate school in human resource development, she was determined to obtain a position in that field. But at age sixty-five, she was also feeling tired. The jobs she found in her newly chosen field would all require a long commute. A workplace close to home was what she wanted. In the end, this was the deciding factor in her accepting a job not precisely in her field, but near home.

Fixed parameters do cut off certain kinds of choices. In so doing, they form a framework for your decisions, point to important choices already made, and provide valuable information about the vocational choices still before you.

EXERCISE

Look over your Practical Parameters Inventory again. List those practical parameters that you cannot or do not choose to change. Beside each parameter listed, write yourself a brief note completing the appropriate sentence (or using words of your own choosing):

- I feel peaceful about this parameter because . . .
- This parameter expresses my commitment to . . .
- This parameter influences my work choice in this way . . .

To enrich what you have done, use the right brain to shine a different light on one or more of the fixed parameters that shape your choices. Think up some metaphors:

- This situation feels like . . .
- . . . reminds me of . . .
- . . . is just like . . .

Have fun with this part of the exercise. What light does humor throw on the situation?

6 Gathering

Purpose: To experience support and feedback as you deal with changing some practical priorities and valuing others; to take stock of where you and your group are in the "working from the heart" process

Everyone bring: Results of activities from Segments 3 and 5

WARM-UP (EVERYONE)
15 MINUTES

Briefly share thoughts and feelings related to doing the exercises in this chapter. You might ask

- What did I learn about myself?
- Do I generally give a lot of or little attention to practical parameters? Do I like the balance I've struck?

SUPPORT AND FEEDBACK (THREES)
20 MINUTES

1. Take turns sharing some of the parameters you want to change, the results you want, and steps you have taken or will take (from Segment 3).
2. Ask for further ideas and feedback. Jot down what seems useful.
3. Ask for ongoing support or accountability in carrying out your steps.

ENCOURAGEMENT AND AFFIRMATION (FOURS)
25 MINUTES

1. Look over the work you did in Segment 5 on the parameters you cannot or choose not to change.
2. Select from this list one you want to talk about.
3. Take turns reading aloud your sentence completions and metaphors for that parameter.

4. Listeners affirm reader's choices and clarity.
5. If there is time, have a free discussion on topics raised.

TAKE STOCK (EVERYONE)
25 MINUTES

Since you have now met together several times, and worked through several chapters alone, this is a good time to take stock of how you are progressing together—and alone. Based on what you discover, make changes in the way you are taking part in your group or partnership.

1. Spend five minutes in silent reflection. Jot down your thoughts related to these questions:
   - How am I doing in the "working from the heart" process?
   - What is working well? Where am I having difficulty?
   - What changes would I like to make?
   - How do I think the group (or the two of us) is working together? What is going well? What are the difficulties?
   - What changes would I like to make?

2. Share reflections with the whole group (each other).

CLOSING (EVERYONE)
5 MINUTES

7 Step Back and Survey

Have you ever flown in a helicopter or a small plane? The experience is both exhilarating and humbling—gazing down on hills, streams, roads, and neighborhoods previously explored on foot.

In a sense, that is the point of this chapter: to encourage you to gain an overview of how you want parameters to influence your vocational choices. To gain perspective, it helps to remove yourself from the niggling details of daily life.

From the ground, parameters can seem like mountains too tall to scale, rivers too wide to cross. From the perspective of your whole life, things look more hopeful. Either you can summon the resources you need to change your situation, or you can recognize that situation for what it is—the product of choices you have made and continue to value.

Stepping back and surveying the contours of your life is not a one-shot deal. Practical parameters shift with the passage of time. When that happens, it helps to use the tools offered here and take stock yet again.

EXERCISE

Take another look at the work you did in the activities for Segments 3 and 5. Based on what you learned in the Gathering session, are there any changes you want to make? When you are satisfied with the steps you plan to take, begin (or continue) to carry them out.

On the Summary Page for this chapter, describe how particular parameters shape your work choices. Also indicate any you want to change.

Summarize the things you learned from this chapter. Bring to the surface questions that remain. How will you deal with these?

Move Toward VOCATIONAL DREAMS

Creative people make connections. Making connections is bringing together seemingly unrelated ideas, objects, or events in a way that leads to a new conception.   Frank Barron

4

1 Invent a Dream

The first three steps toward developing work from the heart deal with gifts, meaning, and parameters. These are depicted as the root system of the Eight Steps Tree, mentioned in the introduction. They are the basics of what we bring to our quest, and they issue forth into the tree trunk, those vocational dreams that best express what we wish our work to be.

This chapter invites us to the next step in our process:

Move toward VOCATIONAL DREAMS.

The chapter's purpose is to help us form and choose the dreams we want to explore (Segments 1 and 2), decide how to investigate them (Segments 3, 4, and 5), and then begin our exploration (Gathering and Segment 7).

Our task is to combine gifts, meaning, and parameters in such a way that we come up with one or more vocational dreams colorful and creative enough to grab our imagination. These could involve enriching present work or finding something different for the future. The first three steps required a look inward to identify the gifts, meaning, and parameters that we wish to incorporate in work. Now a more demanding effort is needed to aggregate what we want to offer, investigate opportunities, and generate options for using what we have in a more satisfying way. It's time to roll up our sleeves and get even more committed to finding work we really want to do.

Frank, a computer programmer at a major airline, has decided to concentrate his option-generating efforts on enriching what he now does. Let's look at how he's proceeding.

Gifts: Part of what Frank has to offer is well used in his company. His excellent mathematical, mechanical, and analytical talents, combined with his people skills and love of solving puzzles, have enabled him to work out complicated computer problems and then to teach users how to operate the equipment.

Meaning: Frank has always been fascinated with what makes people tick. Recently, he became certified in the use of the well-known Myers-Briggs Typology Inventory, which helps people identify personality strengths and weaknesses. His spare time has been filled with learning more about philosophy and psychology. At this point, these are the interests that grab him the most.

Parameters: With a mortgage and two kids in college, Frank feels he must stay in his present job, which produces an adequate and reliable income.

Vocational Dreams: His question is, "How can I continue my current work as a computer programmer at my company and also use the personality training I've received?" As he studies more and talks with people, some dreams are forming:

- Offer courses in personality strengths and weaknesses at work.
- Informally use this new knowledge with individuals at work.
- Talk with managers about how to help people understand personality differences.

Each of these activities could be pursued while holding down his present job.

Unlike Frank, Joyce wanted to do something entirely new. At forty-five, disheartened with her work as a budget analyst for a large government agency, she finally quit. To find a different outlet for her talents and interests, she put on her thinking cap. Here's some of what was running through her mind:

> Everyone was flabbergasted when I left because I was so good at my job. But I was sick of it for several reasons. I was tired of being a boss—it really is lonely at the top; that's not just a cliché. I longed for real friendships on the job, not simply "good working relationships." Also, work with figures can get old. Sure, I was powerful—allocating big sums to various projects—but something was missing.

In her search for the missing pieces, Joyce identified her gifts, but nothing new turned up, just strong skills in business and management that had always been there. She reflected further:

> I longed for beauty—flowers, art, music—the parts of life usually associated with recreation and creativity. The trouble was that I didn't have talent in those fields. Yet my love for them seemed to be increasing. I kept wondering what this was telling me. Then one day I put my love of the arts (*meaning*) together with my management skills (*gifts*), and suddenly it dawned on me—maybe I could explore arts management. With the money I've saved, I can give myself six months to find something new (*parameters*).

Continuing her progression of thought, she added:

> I began to wonder if I could find a way to work more *with* people and not always above or below them. And then I thought that if I worked in a fledgling operation, I might have more of that feeling of being creative and working on a team. These ideas sparked me, and I began to think of people I could talk with about finding a small arts group that could use my management skills (*vocational dream*).

The ability to combine gifts, meaning, and parameters into vocational dreams that "fit" is something that can be cultivated. To practice, begin by focusing on others. Invent a dream for someone else. This we do regularly in our seminars.

One person states the gifts, meaning, and parameters they seek to combine. Then others bombard that person with possible careers. These might not be The Best Fantasy Jobs Ever, but they are a step in the right direction and contain valuable clues that may lead to a more compelling dream.

> **EXERCISE**
>
> To get your juices going, try your own hand at Invent a Dream. Think of a person you know or can imagine knowing. In writing, list for that person at least one gift—one statement that captures their sense of meaning, and one parameter that places limitations on them. Bombard the person with as many careers as you can imagine that would combine their gifts, meaning, and parameters. Be as crazy as you wish. It's only pretend! If time permits, try this exercise more than once. Imagination is strengthened through use.

2 Enticing Options That Capture Your Fancy

Turn the spotlight on you. What are the vocational dreams that combine your gifts, meaning, and parameters? And which would you like to explore now? As already mentioned, these dreams can involve enriching your present job, searching for something different, finding a new position in the same organization—any option that gets your juices running. If it's in your imagination, let it come out and play!

As a dreamer, you've got to watch out for two *bugaboos* that typically discourage or confuse:

Bugaboo 1: You can't think of any vocational dreams that turn you on.

Bugaboo 2: You've got too many dreams and don't know which to chase down.

The good news, if you're plagued by Bugaboo 1, is that your dissatisfaction with your current work is a signal that you *can* imagine something else—you just can't flesh it out. Stir up your imagination. Read a book, talk to some upbeat people, swing upside down from a tree—anything to jiggle your brain. Then imagine "I'd like to be . . ." If you still draw a blank, hire an intuitive person for a day to crank out some possibilities for you.

The good news for the Bugaboo 2 folks is that it is OK to explore several dreams at the same time. Indeed, it may be inappropriate to limit yourself to one. Several vocational parts of yourself may want to blossom, and they'll feel squelched if you choose only one! Get started exploring two or three dreams. Either they'll combine in a way you had not thought about, or one will gather more energy than the others and seem right for now.

If you're nervous about making a "wrong" choice, the good news for you is that you don't have to be right; you just have to be close. Do you remember playing hide and seek, and hinting that the searcher was either "hot," "warm," or "cold"? By tracking down "warm" dreams, you may be led to something really "hot."[1]

EXERCISE

1. Generate one or more vocational dreams in either or both of the following categories:

   Enrich your present work. Dream yourself into an ideal way of doing what you're now doing.

   Find something new. Imagine a way to use the same or different gifts in another arena making the same or different salary. Or allow yourself to be wild and crazy and describe a job that expresses your secret fantasy.

To stimulate your thought, consider these additional questions:

- Do I prefer working with **people, data,** or **things** (or some combination of these)?
- With what **subject** or **issue** would I like to be involved?
- What **skills** do I especially want to use in work?

State the options you think up in an upbeat fashion. Here's what Marge, a grade school teacher, thought about:

- I have a teacher's aide. Together we create learning experiences that help kids recognize the wisdom of twentieth-century geniuses (ideal way of doing present job).
- "I'm a consultant/trainer in corporations, using my teaching skills with adults and making more money than I did in my school job" (same skills, different arena).
- "I've hit the stage as a renowned character actress and teach people about life" (wild and crazy secret fantasy).

To help you generate vocational options, consult both your spontaneous self and your reflective self.

Spontaneous self. Take a walk with a pad and pencil in hand. Take in what you see. Let it feed you. Then ask, "What are my vocational dreams?" Write down gut-level responses. Be as free as possible, even if the idea seems impractical or silly. If you always wanted to be an artist, write that down. Do you have gifts you rarely use and want to develop? Would you like to apply proven skills to a cause you believe in passionately? Maybe you'd like more room for creativity and originality in your present job. You'd like to work fewer hours so that you can have more time for yourself. For now, let reality go out the window. Don't ponder too long; go with your instinctive feeling.

Reflective self. Give yourself time to take a thoughtful look at the work you have done so far with this book. Allow it to help you form and select some dreams to explore.

Spread out your Summary Pages, journal entries, and any other materials you have gathered thus far. If you remember an illuminating dream, write down its essence and place that before you as well.

Quiet your mind. Allow yourself to focus on all these reminders of who you are and what you most want to do with your life.

Then ask, "What are my vocational dreams?" Write or draw something in response.

2. Look at the vocational options you've generated and decide which you want to explore now. Write these in your notebook.

When you've chosen some dreams to explore, post them in a place where you'll run into them—on a mirror, on the fridge, on a counter. Let them percolate for a while. Wear one or two like a new coat. See how that feels.

3 Sleuth Your Way to Clarity

You've chosen one or more dreams to explore. You might have questions such as:

"I wonder whether I could quit my law firm and start my own legal practice?"

"Could I possibly turn my love of photography into a business?"

"If I do community development work, can I find a job that pays the salary I need?"

Most vocational exploration methods boil down to three familiar activities you engage in every day of your life: *talk*, *read*, and *experience*. Which you do and in what combination depends on the kind of person you are and how you learn best.

When Ken wondered if he could start his own law firm, he decided to talk with people who have successfully done that. Hearing about Ken's talks, Betty said, "That might help Ken, but I feel shy talking with people about a topic I'm not sure of. Reading something is the best way for me to start gathering the information I need." Emily realized, "I learn things best through experience. Put me in a situation and let me start doing something. I'll learn once I'm involved."

It's probably good to use all three methods of exploration in some sort of combination. Place the emphasis on what is most motivating to you. Like Sherlock Holmes, collect fragments, clues, bits and pieces of information, and gradually piece them into a meaningful whole.

TALK

Once you focus on something you're interested in and start talking about it, it's surprising how soon and how frequently you run into people who know something about the subject. Returning home from an overseas Peace Corps assignment, Henry, aged twenty-six, thought he'd like to work in city management. At a party, he bumped into a friend who happened to know the manager of a neighboring city. This friend was willing to let Henry use his name in calling for an appointment to meet the manager. Just by telling his friend what he wanted to explore, Henry turned up a promising next step.

In our seminars, we often set up what we call a "resource merry-go-round." On notebook sheets, participants describe the kind of help they need. Then, taking turns, they place these sheets on a chair in the center of the circle, speak about what they need, and invite others in the group to sign their names if they have information to offer. Participants have asked how to:

- boost office morale
- get a different type of work in the same company
- market a book
- institute a recycling program in a company
- do theater with disadvantaged kids
- learn landscape design

Almost always someone in the room has a clue.

You are probably surrounded by people who can help you in your search or who know others who can. Even if talk is not your favorite style of gathering information, consider letting people around you know what you're looking for. You'll obtain useful clues, information, and contacts. Whether or not you follow up on every "helpful" suggestion is up to you.

Once you know someone has information you need, you can make contact in a variety of ways:

- Arrange to meet casually over coffee.
- Set up a ten-minute telephone conference to "pick their brain."
- Schedule twenty to thirty minutes to meet more formally at their place of work.

The type of conversation you'll have is commonly called *interviewing for information*. An invaluable skill that can be used for a variety of purposes, interviewing for information is a way to obtain a lot of information about almost any area you want to explore.

Whether your conversation is casual or more intentional, be conscious of the kind of help you want to receive. Ask questions that will elicit the kind of information you need:

- What kinds of jobs are available in your field for people with skills like mine?
- What are the requirements to qualify for these positions?
- Are there other departments in the company where I might use my skills?
- What are the key conferences people in your field attend that I might participate in to get a feel for this kind of work?
- You've heard what I'm exploring. Are there particular publications or books you would recommend that could take me further?

Interviewing for information has many benefits. From knowledgeable people, you can learn shortcuts to take, a pertinent article to read, or the next person to contact. As you speak with other people, you spark each other to think of ideas neither would have thought up alone. You form a network of successful, well-connected people who know what you're exploring and can give you further tips. Sometimes, you hear about job openings before they are publicly advertised. Though not the primary purpose of interviewing for information, this may be a helpful by-product and, in a tight job market, a useful one.

Read "Interviewing for Information," appendix B, for more tips on how to use this important sleuthing skill.

READ

If talking with people about your quest gives you the jitters, first treat yourself to some quiet exploration through reading. Go to the library, browse in bookstores, write to organizations for literature. The more you look, the more you'll find readings that address your questions. As Barbara Sher writes in her useful book *Wishcraft*, "I'm a great believer in libraries—and in librarians, bless them. You can go to the library in any moderate-sized town, college, or university and find out almost anything you need to know, from the regulations of the American Kennel Club to the Gross National Product of Paraguay."[2]

Tired of the usual office routine, Mac hungered for intellectual challenge to enrich his work. Deadlines and a heavy job load made it unlikely that his office would be scheduling any fascinating seminars. *The Fifth Discipline*, by business writer Peter Senge, came to his attention.[3] Finding it to contain just the challenge he craved, he invited a couple of office mates to read the book with him and then discuss it over lunch once a week.

Pam, upon graduating from college with a degree in therapeutic recreation, wanted to discover the various ways she could work with handicapped people. From the National Information Center for Handicapped Children and Youth, she requested their brochure "Investigating Careers in Service to People with Special Needs." What she found was a gold mine of information available for the price of a postcard.

Many more associations than you imagine are devoted to providing information and resources on specific vocational fields and on specialties within those fields.[4]

EXPERIENCE

Think of experience as falling into two categories: personal exposure and training.

Personal Exposure. This means placing yourself in a work setting where you meet practitioners or join in the actual work. There are a whole range of activities that fall into this category.

If you want an immediate feel for what it is like to work in the training department of your company, ask to **observe** for a day or two with someone in that unit. To experience the photography business, **volunteer** for a short time as an assistant. To live out one of your vocational dreams, you might be able to obtain **temporary work, part-time work,** or **vacation work** (work you do while on vacation). If you are starting out, an **internship position** might provide the experience you need to decide whether to pursue a particular vocational path.

Jennifer, an organic farming student, was not sure about the kind of farm on which she wanted to work. She decided to visit a series of farms, working for three weeks at each one in return for room and board. At the third she met a grower who was starting an agricultural experiment in Mexico. Sensing her enthusiasm, the grower asked Jennifer if she wanted to help in that project. Not only did Jennifer find paid work, she also realized how much agriculture in developing nations interested her.

Another way to get personal experience is to **affiliate** with a professional or vocational organization active in your field. This gives you a chance to associate with people working in your area of interest. By serving with them on committees and task forces, you can try your hand at doing the kind of work you think you might want to do in the future. You also learn of job opportunities and conferences in the field you are investigating.

As you gain hands-on experience, ask yourself,

- How do I like working in this field?
- Do I like the kinds of people who are doing the work I am investigating?
- Do I like the projects they undertake?

Training. The second category of experience is training that will teach you more about the vocational aspirations you are investigating.

Here are some ways to test the waters:
- **Workshops and conferences** require a minimum investment of time, energy, and money and are usually packed with useful information and

activities. They teach skills, facilitate networking, and offer tested resources.

- **Short continuing education courses** introduce you to more formal education in the area you are investigating. An initial taste helps you decide whether you want more education or not. Find out if the material of the course energizes you or puts you to sleep.

If after careful investigation, a full academic or vocational program seems to be the next step, be sure to choose the program wisely. Ask if it will prepare you to realize your working goal. Check the reputation of the school, the department, and the faculty.

It is surprising how often people think of obtaining a graduate degree in order to see what kind of work they want to do. Graduate work has its place, but do some careful investigation before jumping into such a large commitment of time and money.

Finding the best training to fit your particular needs is worth the time it takes to do it. A good training decision can take you far along your vocational path. A poor one wastes time and money and causes discouragement. More thoughts on training are included in appendix C.

However you investigate your vocational dreams—through talking, reading, experience, or a combination of the three—it's important to frame good questions, such as the ones suggested in the section "Talk." These evolve as you gain new information.

EXERCISE

For each dream you're exploring, create a notebook page. Describe the dream. Then list the questions you need answered to pursue it.

Then for each dream, create three sections headed *Talk*, *Read*, and *Experience*. Brainstorm as many ideas as possible about people to talk with, reading to consider, and experiences to try. Write them in the appropriate spaces. These are resource lists for your investigation.

This is a beginning. Update and modify your lists as you think of new questions and gather new information.

4 Plan Your Investigation

When Tish Sommers was forming the Older Women's League (OWL), one of her favorite sayings was "Organize, don't agonize."[5] That's terrific advice for us. Organize for action! Plan specific steps to take within a given time frame to investigate your dream. Call this your Vocational Exploration Plan. Create one for each dream you want to look into. Include the vocational dream you intend to explore, plus a few steps to get moving.

Most people, once they get started, make a series of Vocational Exploration Plans, either on paper or in their minds, each one building on the last as their knowledge of the area they're investigating becomes clearer.

Take Henry, whom we met in Segment 3. He decided to explore the field of city management. You may recall that a friend put Henry in contact with the manager of a neighboring city. From talking with this person, Henry learned about training requirements and job opportunities in the field. He also found out that the International Association of City Managers lists job openings in its journal.

There he found many positions requiring a master's degree. This he did not have and did not currently want to obtain. However, he also noticed that smaller towns were willing to hire managers for a lower salary and with fewer educational requirements. This suited him well.

Once he focused in and began telling others what he was looking for, people began calling him. His cousin told him about a position in Virginia; an old work buddy from Maine described an opening he knew about. Henry decided to visit Vermont to interview for several openings. Other people came up with additional leads. His mood changed. He no longer felt discouraged. "Now I have confidence that there's a job out there that's right for me. But it's going to take work, patience, and perseverance to find it."

Henry's story is still unfolding. A month ago he was in a fog about the future. Now he has direction and is on his way. *Each step led to another.* His evolving Vocation Exploration Plans, which he constructed in his head, would have looked like this in writing:

Vocational Exploration Plan 1
Dream to explore: city management
Steps: 1. Talk with city manager—Nov. 28
         2. Read material in her office—Nov. 28

Vocational Exploration Plan 2

Dream to explore: city management
Steps: 1. Talk with city management association—Dec. 1
2. Read material in that office—Dec. 1

Vocational Exploration Plan 3

Dream to explore: small-town management
Steps: 1. Go to Vermont—Dec. 10
2. Talk with as many people as possible about how to break into smalltown management—Dec. 10–14

Well, you get the idea. Now it's your turn.

> **EXERCISE**
>
> On a notebook page, create a blank form (or several forms) for your Vocational Exploration Plan like the one that follows. On this form, name the vocational dream you wish to investigate. In Segment 3, you created a list of questions plus three resource lists headed *Read, Talk, Experience*. Review these resource lists, and circle several items that seem most doable now. That will get the ball rolling. Enter these as steps on your Vocational Exploration Plan form. Be as specific as possible. Put a date next to each. Label this your Vocational Exploration Plan.

Vocational Exploration Plan

Dream to Explore:
Steps: (Action/Date)

1. _____
2. _____
3. _____

> As you think through your Vocational Exploration Plan, you (like Henry) may become aware that you need a particular kind of help for which you don't have any resources. List specific kinds of help you need. Resolve to talk with two people who either can give you the help you need or might know of someone else who can help.

5 Start Easy

To get rolling with your Vocational Exploration Plan, make your first step something that is not too demanding. That way, you will bring a good measure of confidence and clarity as you **read, talk,** and **experience** your way toward your dream.

If you have a case of the jitters as you contemplate seeking information from others, perhaps you're thinking too big. For example, if you want to break into car manufacturing, it's great to think of strolling into the office of the president of the Ford Motor Company and announcing that you're ready to take over. But that's not the place to start!

Begin as Henry did by talking casually with friends about your dreams. See who has clues for you. If the library has shelves of books on car manufacturing—how to build cars, the pros and cons of Japanese versus American models, and the technicalities of emission control, look for the most readable one to get you started—perhaps Lee Iacocca's autobiography. Or check the magazine section for short articles.

If a bird jumps on your shoulder and squawks in your ear, "Don't ask stupid questions!" just tell it to calm down. No questions are really stupid. You *know* that. But in case you still hear the bird whispering, show the questions you have in mind to a friend. Get some feedback.

To start off any inquiry, state clearly where you are, where you'd like to go, and what you need to know. Here's what Jim, a recent college graduate, stated:

> I've just graduated with a civil engineering degree and would like to get into automobile manufacturing. I'm looking for an overview of the industry, the types of jobs available, and how to break in at the entry level.

That statement, simple as it sounds, is tough to create. It takes a lot of thought to be concise. We call it a Where I Am/Want to Go Statement (Am/Go Statement for short).

Toni, a lawyer for the city of Memphis, enjoys much of her job. A nature lover and trained musician, she keeps trying to feed those parts of herself during her off hours, but she can find little time for this.

"It would be great if I could find a way to incorporate music and nature on the job." Recently she has started telling people about her dream and asking for ideas.

Here's her Am/Go Statement:

> As lawyer for the city of Memphis, I'm in a job I want to keep. I'd like to enrich it through bringing nature and music into what I do. I'm looking for ideas on how to do that.

As far-fetched as that sounds, Toni found people in her organization with musical interests. When it came time for an office party, they put together a wacky musical spoof. The whole effort brought a sense of fun that picked up everyone's spirits. To feed her nature-lover's soul, she takes lunchtime walks through the city park.

EXERCISE

Put together your own Am/Go Statement by thinking through this outline:

- Current job or status
- Vocational dream you're exploring
- What you need to know

Then create your statement. Speak it aloud a few times. Polish it up. Then try it out with a friend. Ask for feedback: is it clear?

6 Gathering

Purpose: To practice interviewing for information; to describe your Vocational Exploration Plan 1 and to obtain help on it

Everyone bring:

Am/Go Statement from Segment 5

Vocational Exploration Plan 1 from Segment 4

List of help you need from Segment 4

WARM-UP (EVERYONE)
10 MINUTES

Briefly check with each other on how it felt to choose a vocational dream. Everyone share a word or two.

INTERVIEW FOR INFORMATION (TWOS)
40 MINUTES

Randomly get into pairs. You will be practicing an informal kind of interviewing for information with your partner. It is like a spontaneous conversation you might have with the person next to you at a party, on a bus, at a child's soccer game. Use your Am/Go Statement to tell where you are and what you hope for as a dream vocation. Then ask your questions. See what you can learn "on the spot" from your partner. You may be surprised at how much help you can surface in a ten- or fifteen-minute conversation.

- Interview (fifteen minutes): Interviewer asks questions.
- Debrief (five minutes): Exchange information on how the interviewing went and what could be improved.
- Repeat the process, reversing roles (fifteen-minute interview, five-minute debriefing).

ENCOURAGEMENT AND HELP (EVERYONE)
15 MINUTES

1. Share your Vocational Exploration Plan.

2. Name the help you need.

3. Those who have ideas about how to help should raise their hands. Record these responses for contacting later. If there is time, hear their ideas now. (If you are doing this exercise with a partner, exchange your lists and brainstorm possible resources.)

4. After everyone has shared, send each other off with words of encouragement.

CLOSING (EVERYONE)
5 MINUTES

---

7 Listen to Your Dreams

You've chosen one or more dreams to explore, learned ways to investigate them, selected specific steps to begin. As you begin exploring, you might feel excited or a bit nervous. Perhaps a bit of both.

Defining what constitutes meaningful work is like shopping for clothes or records or books. Some people love the open-ended search. Others don't. Either way, the name of the game is to try things on—clothing, musical tastes, literary genres. A good shopper will tell you to try on what immediately appeals, but also to experiment. That's the way to get to know yourself better. "Oh no! This is too bright on me." "Hey, I didn't know I liked jazz!" "What an extraordinary poet; I'd never heard of her."

For some, an invitation to shop is a chance to relax and have fun. It's a no-risk proposition for uninhibited expression and trying new things. For others, the prospect is slightly more appealing than a ten-year jail sentence. For these folks, so much to choose from and no real way to make a choice is a curse.

Know who you are. If vocational exploration comes easy, celebrate that fact and enjoy the experience. If it comes hard, know that the reward is sweet and solid when it comes.

In this chapter you've been challenged to choose an occupational dream to explore. No one is saying that this is what you will end up doing for the rest of your life. In choosing a dream to investigate—any dream—you are taking a valuable step. You are learning how to explore a field of interest and to gain information. Your Vocational Exploration Plan is an unfolding, evolving document. Completion of one step gives birth to ten new ideas on how to proceed. Let the energy you feel as you finish one step motivate you to articulate and complete the next steps.

Talk with friends and with professionals active in the field you're considering, read relevant writings, and taste experientially that which you think you might want to do. Not only will your plan evolve, but the very way you think about your future work may grow or shift. Don't resist this process; embrace it. It means you are getting closer.

If you're exploring several vocational dreams, as mentioned before, it is likely that one might gather energy as you look into it or that two or more might combine in a form you had not expected.

Pat was a room-service waiter at a hotel chain but had dreams of moving up. First he thought his organization skills might qualify him to manage the room-service operation. But he also likes bookkeeping and accounting and thought he'd try to move into that department. Gradually, however, his interest in the environment deepened. He found himself reading all he could find on recycling. This inspired him to propose a recycling operation for his company with You Know Who to head it up. Yes, it was accepted. Now Pat is using organizational, management, and accounting abilities in a cause he really believes in.

You may have dreams that can't be expressed in work now. They are not yet fully developed or you cannot find a market for them. These are minority voices—don't neglect them!

Alfredo, a manager in a trade association, has long enjoyed gourmet cooking and dreamed of opening his own restaurant. Forty years of age with lots of family expenses, he is in no position to leave his present job. Away from work, however, he nurtures his dream. An avid recipe collector, he enjoys nothing more than preparing creative meals for good friends. Eventually, he hopes to make a living at it.

Sometimes a dream will occur to you that seems outlandish. But if it stays with you, pay attention to it, and give it room to play. Maria, an editor for a publishing company, dreams of being a character actress. Right now that character actress in her is like a small, undeveloped child; she has only performed in one play. But Maria is giving her actress self lots of loving attention—taking acting classes, reading and attending plays, practicing monologues, auditioning, working behind the scenes in productions. Gradually, the actress part of herself is gaining confidence. It will grow and perhaps one day be large and strong enough to take over her work life.

If you have several vocational dreams, you have several options: combine them in work now, select one to work on now but feed another so that will gradually grow, or express one or more in your spare time.

One last tip: don't run out of steps to take in your exploration. Always have a few in your hip pocket. Why? If one strategy doesn't pan out the way you'd hoped, having another can help you recoup more easily. It's like the wise writer who always has another copy of her manuscript addressed and ready to send to another publisher if, as will happen, the mail brings a rejection notice. Some steps lead nowhere. Expect that. When it happens, go back to the fork in the road and take another route toward realizing your vocational dreams.

EXERCISE

Contact those who offered help during the Gathering session to obtain their ideas. Incorporate into your Vocational Exploration Plan any modifications that occur to you as a result of the session.

Enter the dreams you are exploring on the Summary Page of this chapter.

Begin or continue to carry out your Vocational Exploration Plan. Reflect on the progress you've made.

Summarize your learnings from this chapter. What further questions do you have?

Identify PEOPLE to Help

Very few people ever make it alone. We all need someone to lead the way, to show us the ropes, to tell us the norms, to encourage, support, and make it a little easier for us. Who are these people who will do that and where do we find them? They have been called benefactors, godfathers, patrons, rabbis. Natasha Josefowitz

1 People Power

"Without him I could not be doing what I'm doing,"[1] said a graduate at the death of Father Gilbert Hartke, founder of the Speech and Drama Department at The Catholic University of America. Known for taking students under his wing throughout their university training and well afterward, Father Hartke taught, coached, and directed; he probed, prodded, and cheered. With his loving attention, his students were encouraged to do their best.

When searching for work or enriching what you now do, don't expect to do it alone. Get help from others. By yourself you can get only so far. With other people's help you can get much further. In chapter 4, we looked to others primarily for information. Now we will expand our understanding of how people can assist us by exploring the ongoing help we need. We turn to the next key step:

Identify PEOPLE to help.

We'll begin by remembering how we've helped others in the past, how others have given us aid, and the importance that has had for us (Segment 1). This is followed by a view of the various types of help people can offer and a chance to identify which types of help we need now (Segment 2). Next, we'll identify who can give us this assistance (Segment 3). Then we will examine how to receive wisdom from inner companions who can act as our guides (Segment 4). Next, we will decide our next move related to seeking help from others (Segment 5). Finally, Segment 7 discusses the importance of forming a personal network of support.

At Christmas, a card came with these words written by Helen Keller, who was blind, deaf, and mute:

> . . .the best and most beautiful
>
> things in the world
>
> cannot
>
> be seen nor even touched,
>
> but just
>
> felt in the heart.[2]

As a child, Helen's unrelenting temper tantrums had been the despair of her friends and family. What brought her to the place where she could write such tender thoughts? Crucial to her development was the loving, careful instruction offered by her teacher, Annie Sullivan. Also handicapped, Annie believed in the possibilities that resided within Helen, the seemingly hopeless case that was her charge.

People who believe in us—the Annie Sullivans, the Gilbert Hartkes, Scout leaders, coaches, teachers, parents, grandparents—encourage and energize us to do work that draws on our best self: work that is first and foremost felt in the heart. We, also, can be the Annie Sullivan or Gilbert Hartke to others, believing in their potential and helping them to make their way.

In the preface to one of her books, *In Search of Our Mothers' Gardens,* Alice Walker puts it beautifully:

> In my development as a human being and as a writer I have been, it seems to me, extremely blessed, even while complaining. Wherever I have knocked, a door has opened. Wherever I have wandered, a path has appeared. I have been helped, supported, encouraged, and nurtured by people of all races, creeds, colors, and dreams; and I have, to the best of my ability, returned help, support, encouragement, and nurture. This receiving, returning, or passing on has been one of the most amazing, joyous, and continuous experiences of my life.[3]

Each of us is part of this network of encouragement. All we have to do is realize this and act on it. Keep in mind a chain reaction: "I help you; you help another; that one reaches to still another." That releases us from the burden of "tit for tat": "How can I ask someone for help if I have not done a favor for them?" When we realize how much we help others along their way, it is easier to approach people with our own wish for assistance. We are also strengthened by remembering the people who have nurtured us thus far.

EXERCISE

In your notebook begin a list of the helpers who have made you what you are. Look around you. Reach back in time. Enjoy remembering each one who comes to mind. Draw again on the energy they have given you as you record their names.

Create a similar list of the people you have helped on their way.

Become conscious of the role of helpful people in the lives of those you know or hear about. Remember Geraldine Ferraro naming Tip O'Neill as her mentor? Or Florence Griffith-Joyner attributing her Olympic success to the encouragement of her husband? Keep an eye out for examples like this. They'll encourage you to offer and to ask for the support you need.

2 A Variety of Help Is Available

Open your eyes to the many types of assistance we can offer one another in pursuit of fulfilling work. That expands your horizons as to the kind of encouragement you could receive from outside yourself.

When Joseph Campbell, mentioned in chapter 1, was asked, "Do you ever have this sense when you are following your bliss . . . of being helped by hidden hands?" he replied,

> All the time. It is miraculous. I even have a superstition that has grown on me as the result of invisible hands coming all the time—namely, that if you do follow your bliss you put yourself on a kind of track that has been there all the while, waiting for you, and the life that you ought to be living is the one you are living. When you can see that, you begin to meet people who are in the field of your bliss, and they open doors to you. I say, follow your bliss and don't be afraid, and doors will open where you didn't know they were going to be.[4]

Yes, doors will open. But we must do our share of knocking. And not just on one door, but on several.

Think of mentoring, for example. According to Margo Murray, an expert on mentoring, a study of prominent male and female executives revealed that nearly "two-thirds of those surveyed reported having had a mentor or sponsor."[5] Murray quotes the study itself: "Executives who have had a mentor earned more money at a younger age, . . . are happier with their progress and derive greater pleasure from their work."[6]

You might like to have a mentor. If you are clear about wanting one, you may be closer than you think to finding someone who could give you the mentoring you need. At this point our purpose is to understand that mentoring is one of many kinds of help people can offer. There are several others.

To gain flexibility and save on office overhead expenses, Bruce moved his public relations business into his home. The first year he loved being away from the hustle and bustle of office interaction. But gradually the spark left his

Identify PEOPLE to Help

work. Finally, he admitted, "I'm lonely. I miss having colleagues to bounce things around with."

"I've got an idea for a new product I'd like to develop for my company," said Carol, "but I need advice on the technical details."

Bruce looked for colleagues. Carol wanted advice. Both identified something they needed from others. They did not know who could give it. They only wished someone could.

The following People Help Inventory will stimulate you to differentiate the kinds of assistance you need.

> **EXERCISE**
>
> ### PEOPLE HELP INVENTORY
>
> *Directions: As you read each section in the People Help Inventory, check which are relevant or irrelevant for you at this point in your quest. Don't worry about being right or being thorough; and don't think through the implications of your choices. Be spontaneous. If you wish you had such help now, the kind of help described is relevant. If the description doesn't ring a bell, it's irrelevant. In your notebook, list the types of assistance that seem relevant to you now, assistance that you need to move forward. This list is likely to change and evolve.*
>
> **Colleague:** Someone to work with or an associate in a similar profession.
>
> *Wish:*
> "I work all alone; I need colleagues."
> "I'd like to have lunch with someone in the same business with whom I could unwind and brainstorm ideas."
>
> *Possibility:*
> Nan and Terry both work in alternative health care, Nan as a nurse-healer, Terry as a massage therapist. Each works independently, but they look to each other for support and information on shared issues: how to deal with problem clients, what companies to use for advertising, where to locate their offices.
>
> ☐ Relevant   ☐ Irrelevant

Mentor: Someone who believes in you and offers guidance and coaching to help you move forward.

Wish:

"I've always wished someone would take an interest in my progress as I develop my career."

"I need support from someone who has contacts, influence, and faith in my abilities and who can open some doors for me or point out opportunities."

Possibility:

A writer in the beginning stages of his career, Pedro asked a published author to read his work. Feeling it had merit, the author encouraged him, answered questions, and suggested useful writing seminars.

☐ Relevant   ☐ Irrelevant

Supervisor: Someone to oversee your work and guarantee its quality by the strength of his or her credentials and expertise.

Wish:

"As a counselor, my next step is to obtain supervision so I can be certified."

"I'm preparing food in my restaurant according to the theory advanced by a particular nutritionist. I'd like to meet with her once a week for a while until I'm sure I'm doing things right."

Possibility:

As a volunteer, Karin, trained in art history, offered to write the catalog for a museum exhibit. She asked the curator to supervise her work. Later, when applying for a paid position in art history, her supervisor's recommendation opened the door to employment.

☐ Relevant   ☐ Irrelevant

Adviser: Knowledgeable person who offers information and counsel.

Wish:

"I wish I knew someone who could tell me what professional organization I should join."

"I'd like to find someone who can advise me on where to find job listings in my field."

"Is it necessary to join the union in order to break into the field? I'd love to talk to someone who really knows this stuff."

Identify PEOPLE to Help

Possibility:
Barry wants to prepare for international development work. He contacted Jane, a Foreign Service officer, to ask for her advice on the requirements needed to break into the field. "There are three," she said, "fluency in a major language, two years overseas living experience, and a master's degree in a field that is used overseas."

☐ Relevant   ☐ Irrelevant

Collaborator: A person with whom you want to produce something. This can involve anything from a legal working partnership to an occasional productive association.

Wish:
"I am most effective when working as part of a team."
"I have the technical skills to create my invention but want to find someone with marketing and financial expertise to package it for buyers."

Possibility:
A talented young New York architect, Pierre wanted to start his own firm. The problem? "I can design houses," he said, "but I can't find people who need houses designed. What I'm looking for is someone good at architectural marketing with whom I can join forces."

Pierre thought of two possibilities for collaboration: his friend Rosa, strong in marketing, with whom he might go into business, and Ted, whose public relations and marketing firm might generate clients for Pierre.

☐ Relevant   ☐ Irrelevant

Role model: Someone who does what I would like to do or who inspires me in my work.

Wish:
"I'd like to know someone who has successfully walked this same difficult road before me."
"I'm juggling multiple roles—schoolteacher, single parent, and prime care giver for my aging mother. It would be great to talk with somebody who's done this kind of thing well."

Possibility:
"Dr. Martin Luther King, Jr., has been my lifelong inspiration," says Al, a police officer. "Everything he has written, I have read. When I'm feeling discouraged, I return to Dr. King's writings. They give me strength. His struggles motivate my sense of mission."

☐ Relevant   ☐ Irrelevant

Friend: A person in whom you can confide your vocational hopes and dreams, failures and successes.

Wish:

"I feel like letting off steam—I'm so confused. I'd like to share what I'm going through with someone who will listen and help me sort through my feelings."

"I got a wild idea last night—I'd like to start my own business. I need to toss this idea around with someone just to hear how it sounds out loud."

Possibility:

Just before Jill drove off for an important job interview, the phone rang. It was Greg. "I'll be thinking of you as you go through the interview. I know you'll do a great job. Be sure to call me after it's over. I'm dying to hear what happened." This was not the first time this had occurred. Greg, of all her friends, had supported Jill through the stops and starts of her vocational meanderings. He was really interested. Jill felt it and was grateful.

☐ Relevant   ☐ Irrelevant

Teacher: Someone to impart knowledge or offer training in skills you need; this can involve anything from Annie Sullivan's intense relationship with Helen Keller to getting tips from an office mate over a cup of coffee.

Wish:

"My new computer baffles me. I don't have time for a whole course. I'd like someone to sit down with me for a couple of hours to get me started."

"People have told me for years that my writing is awful. I'm determined to write well. I'm looking for a teacher who will be really patient with me."

Possibility:

Chuck knew that his colleague Meg had attended a seminar on meeting facilitation and was eager to share her knowledge, so he invited her over for the evening to share her new learnings. This gave Meg a chance to solidify what she had been taught, and Chuck got some new information to strengthen his own skills.

☐ Relevant   ☐ Irrelevant

Patron: Someone to value your work, support it or become a consumer of it, and pass the word about it to others.

Wish:

"I love creating my paintings. What I don't love is finding people to buy them and exposing them to others."

Possibility:

We frequently see people acting as patrons for artists. For example, hairdressers Ken and Evelyn invited their customer Pat to display her watercolors in their shop. That was a way to give them exposure.

Patroning can occur in other fields as well. When Dick wanted to get into the taxi business, his Uncle Bob loaned him money for his first cab. Dick had found a patron.

☐ Relevant   ☐ Irrelevant

Spiritual guide: Someone to support your spiritual quest and care how that is expressed in work; this could be a friend wise in spiritual ways or a clergyperson or someone specially trained to offer spiritual companionship to others.[7]

Wish:

"I don't find meaning in my work any more. I wish I could find someone to talk with about this."

"I want to develop an active spiritual life even though I'm not particularly religious. Classes are not enough. I need a coach."

"Spirituality is important to me. I'd like it to carry over into my work, but I need help in figuring how."

Possibility:

Bill learned about a nearby spiritual formation center that trains people to offer spiritual guidance. Through the center, he obtained names of several people who could offer the spiritual companionship he was looking for.

☐ Relevant   ☐ Irrelevant

Include any additional types of assistance you need to move toward more meaningful work.

3 Who Can Fit the Bill?

Several kinds of assistance might be useful to us now. But where to find those who can give us the help we need? This is where creativity kicks in. Imagine snorkeling in a clear, sparkling lagoon teeming with exotic fish, strange of hue and shape. Suddenly you're eyeball to eyeball with a great white shark. Tickling its chin, you say, "Hello, I need your help. Could you lead me to the sunken treasure?"

A bit zany? Not really. The fact is, most of us swim in a huge pool with dozens of talented people all around us who are not only willing but happy to help us on our way. The problem is, we just don't know it, because we've got blinders on and see only those right in front of us as potential helpers.

Instead of simply crying, "Heeelllppp!" think more specifically about what kind of aid would be most helpful. Then, in brainstorming fashion, imagine all the people who could possibly lend a hand. For example, you want to get your courage up to ask for a raise. You might confide this desire to a friend in order to get used to speaking about it. And you might turn to your colleague Bill who just got a raise to hear how he did it. Or you could visit your firm's personnel department to learn more about the salary structure where you work. Probably all these approaches would help you gain courage, clarity, and the specific information needed to make an informed request for a salary increase.

Sometimes help comes spontaneously as you speak about your vocational dreams. In one of our seminars, Jane, in her thirties and dissatisfied with her job as a diplomat's administrative support person, blurted out, "You know what I'd really like to do? I'd like to be an actress and an ambassador to Italy!" One participant quickly replied, "I can see that. Shirley Temple Black did it. Maybe you could too!" Another added, "And think of Clare Boothe Luce. She *was* ambassador to Italy!" Quicker than she had time to think about it, Jane had two role models whose lives she could investigate for clues.

Will that lead her to an ambassadorial position? Who knows? What's important now is that Jane can picture two people who combined what she would like to do. As she learns about Luce and Temple Black, all sorts of other possibilities might present themselves.

Sometimes you have to work to find the help you need. Jack wanted to leave his corporate management position to try his hand at cabinetmaking. He knew this required a leap to find out if it would be truly satisfying—and lucrative enough. So he set up shop in his garage. On weekends, he turned out finely crafted furniture and sold it to friends.

His first efforts piqued his interest, but also led him to conclude that if he were really to make a living, he'd have to invest in more tools. Visiting a couple of skilled cabinetmakers, he observed their equipment. One told him of a local bank that finances small business start-ups. While there he learned about the Small Business Administration's Senior Corps of Retired Executives (SCORE), which provides ongoing expertise to small entrepreneurs. His local SCORE representative was full of advice about how to create a business plan, apply for local licenses, and market products. All this was given without cost.

The people you know can often lead you to those more removed from your circle, those who can perhaps offer more expert assistance than you could find by yourself. This is obviously what happened in Jack's case.

So take those blinders off. Look widely for the help you need. Start, of course, with your inner circle—friends, relatives, colleagues—people you know personally. Then dream more expansively. "If only I could speak with . . . , I could . . ." Now think of someone who could lead you to that person.

One caution goes almost without saying. Don't expect one poor soul to give you all the ideas and encouragement you need. They'll sink with the burden. This is what happened to Sally, Jack's wife, before he reached out to others.

As he explored his new career in cabinetmaking, Jack continually asked Sally to listen to his ideas and to help him decide how to proceed. One evening this set off a flood of irritation in Sally, who replied, "You're expecting too much from me. I have to write a report for work, cook dinner, and clean the apartment. That's too much!" Sally was frustrated and angry. Her husband's vocational search was getting on her nerves. Jack not only wanted her to shoulder more housework and child care along with her job as a graphic artist but also wanted her advice and ideas for his quest.

"But I need your support," protested Jack. He did need Sally's support—but was it fair to ask her for *all* the assistance he required?

"I'm doing my best to take care of housework and kids," she said. "Is it too much to ask that you look elsewhere for vocational counseling?"

Of course not. Though upset by Sally's confrontation, Jack realized she had a point. He began to think about what he needed: "I've got to take stock of where I am. It would be good to talk this through with someone other than Sally who can understand my concerns."

On his part, Jack realized the importance of spreading out his requests for assistance. "Yes, I was expecting too much of Sally. But I also was embarrassed to ask for help from others. Now I realize that when I'm clear about what I need, people are usually more than willing to help."

Specific, well-thought-out requests are likely to bear fruit. You'll find that most people enjoy sharing their expertise. Far from imposing on them, you're honoring the progress they've made by asking them to assist your own.

EXERCISE

Review your list of the types of help you need. For each, create a People Help page. Then brainstorm the names of all those who could give that assistance or could lead you to someone who can.

People Help

I need a _____
   (teacher, mentor, etc.)

The help I need from this person is _____
_____

People who might fill this role are: _____
_____
_____

Let some of these "people help" ideas percolate awhile before carrying them out. We'll return to them in Segment 5.

4 Support from the Inside

To reach the people we've talked about so far requires a call or a note. There is a whole other bank of talent to which we have immediate access—through

Identify PEOPLE to Help

imagination. It is made up of all those people, personally known or unknown, whom we admire.

In his book *Inner Companions*, the syndicated columnist Colman McCarthy writes, "If we can travel with a band of inner companions, what tests can prove too demanding? . . . We need them to share with us the wisdom of the obvious . . . this wisdom must be absorbed into us by opening our interior lives—an intimacy of the spirit."[8]

Your *inner* companions—friends, ancestors, famous people—are loaded with gifts to help your quest. They have wisdom to share.

"My Grandfather Hall's words to me, 'When you make a piece of furniture, finish off all the parts—even those you don't see' are a continuing motto in my life," says Chris, a computer programmer. "Although he died ten years ago, just calling him to mind brings me something special. It makes me realize how important it is to do careful work to meet my own high standards, not just what my organization needs." Grandfather Hall resides within Chris as an ever-available presence to inspire and instruct.

Having been laid off from his job, Art saw an opportunity. "Now I can find what I really want," he exclaimed. That was a year ago. Now after chasing dozens of job leads, he was feeling stuck and wished for encouragement from someone who knew what that was like. "I'm bogged down," he explained. "I have a whole list of things to do and don't want to do any of them." Art found himself thinking of his former neighbor Fred, now living in distant Thailand. Fred had also had a hard time finding work and is now self-employed as an industrial engineer. Thinking about how Fred had weathered a rough period of unemployment made Art think he could too.

EXERCISE

Simply thinking about a person like Grandfather Hall or Fred gives you a boost. But to gain more wisdom, guidance, or inspiration from an inner companion, have an imaginary conversation with that person. No, that's not a crazy thing to do!

For a moment, put aside your doubts. Imagine you're a playwright about to create a dialogue between you and the person you want to learn from. Art decided to do this with Fred. First, bring the person to mind, remembering their special qualities. This is how Art did it:

I'd like to tap into Fred's wisdom. He cares about people, has known tough times, does excellent work, copes with bouts of discouragement. I wonder what he would say to me? I think I'll tell him how I feel.

Then write a conversation in dialogue form. This is what Art wrote:

ART: Fred, I'm really stuck on this job search. I was excited about a possible offer, but when it fell through, I felt horrible. I know I should continue contacting people, but all I feel like doing is being alone, working around the yard, and not talking with anyone.

FRED: Yeah, I know how you feel. I've experienced that many times before.

ART: But what did you do about it? How did you bounce back?

FRED: It wasn't that easy. There were times when it seemed like I was in a cave—it was dark, and I just couldn't see light.

ART: Yeah, that's the way I feel now.

FRED: There were times when I had to face the fact that I couldn't *do* anything more. I had to wait it out. You're probably doing the best thing you can—getting outside, giving your brain a rest, doing physical labor.

ART: Yes, but I feel so useless.

FRED: You might feel that way, but you may be doing something very useful—letting your thoughts and impressions percolate awhile.

ART: I know that can be a good thing to do, that it's important to let things jell, but I still feel useless.

FRED: Is that telling you something?

ART: Maybe it means that there are other ways to be useful than just concentrating too hard on this search.

FRED: Why don't you think about that?

When you set up a dialogue in this fashion, sometimes "new" wisdom or courage is given. Try it once or a few times and see what happens. Here are the steps:

- Become conscious of how you are feeling at this point in your search.
- Think about someone who would understand these feelings and be able to offer wisdom.
- Write a brief description of that person. Why do you want to talk to that person now?

- Imagine the person is with you. Take a few minutes to be conscious of being with the person.
- Then, like Art did, begin a written dialogue with the person. Start by describing your thoughts and feelings about your quest for meaningful work.
- Be quiet and wait for the response of the other person. Write that down.
- Go back and forth—your statement, the other person's response—until you sense that it is finished.
- Read the dialogue you have written. Add more dialogue if it occurs to you.
- Add your reflections and insights about what you have written if you wish.

Summarize what was revealed through the dialogue, and place it in your notebook where it is most applicable.

Try this exercise with different kinds of people. Experiment. The sky's the limit. Just think, it doesn't cost a cent! If you don't have time for a full conversation or written dialogue, call to mind a special person and simply enjoy their presence. Let them be your unseen friend for a while. Whether you write a dialogue or simply think about that other person, you will be enriched by their companionship and perspective.

5 Decide Your Next Move

By now you should have in mind several potential helpers who might assist your progress. Which will you approach? When? How? For what purpose? Focus on the types of assistance that will move you forward at this juncture and the people who can give it.

In her article "Jobless at 61: A Success Story," Carol Van Sickle writes that when her job as an Equal Employment Opportunity officer was abolished, she was tempted to panic. Instead, she created lists. "List number one was of the what-next variety: check retirement picture . . . request leave of absence . . . unemployment benefits?"[9] Finding that the benefits were low, she knew she needed to buy time. So she requested a leave of absence, an option for employees whose jobs were abolished.

Her second list had to do with dissecting her job and proposing how it could be decentralized among various divisions in her organization. It then dawned on her that she could market her skills to another division in the company, the biggest user of her services.

At this point she reached for help. She wanted to know what to expect emotionally as she evolved a strategy to convince the company that she was the right person. Calling a friend whose job had also recently been abolished, she was given this tip: "You're going to feel as if you're on a roller coaster. One minute you'll be flying . . . the next minute you'll be in the pits. . . . But keep all that 'pits' stuff to yourself; or if you feel like crying, call me. You've got to stay *up* every minute, or people will cross the street to avoid you."[10]

Another friend suggested that she could choose whether to be a victim or a product of the downsizing. Determined to be a product, she put fear aside and projected a positive demeanor.

Then she consulted colleagues to help her shape a proposal for a new position. "When you're working out a critical strategy, there's nothing like being surrounded by people who want to help and have good ideas," she discovered. "My proposal went through draft after draft, tightening and sharpening as it went; and when it was pronounced fit, I had no doubt that it was."

EXERCISE

Looking at your own situation, ask yourself what help from someone else would move you off the dime right now. Some advice about where to look for information, a personal introduction to a knowledgeable person, some collaborative help in getting a proposal together? Like Carol, do you have homework you need to do before you approach someone else?

Next, be limited in what you request. As Carol Van Sickle suggests from her experience, "People like to help, but only to the extent they can. When you ask for help, think small and specific."[11] Then choose the person who can respond most immediately—someone accessible, easy to approach. Give that person a call or drop them a note—let a friend know you'd like to be introduced.

Go with the clarity you have. Sometimes just one step is clear. Only when you take it will the next be apparent.

Identify PEOPLE to Help

Suppose you'd like advice on how to create a business from your marble collecting hobby, and no one comes to mind. Not to worry. You've done one great thing—named your need. That's progress. Picture that need as the empty cup carried by the organ-grinder's monkey. Hold it out wherever you go. Watch. Coins will drop in. You'll collect clues and ideas that gradually will lead you forward. By articulating what you want, you alert your unconscious mind to be on the lookout for appropriate assistance. In time it will come.

As a reminder, draw an empty cup, stating one particular kind of help you need from another person. Put this in your wallet so you'll carry it everywhere. Notice when the coins drop in.

If you feel hesitant about asking a particular person for help, consider the following:

- What is the source of your hesitation? Are there ways to recognize your concerns without letting them get the upper hand?
- Are there intermediate steps you can take before you approach a person for support—perhaps have someone introduce you informally?
- Are there ways to find out about the person before you meet?
- Could someone else who does not make you feel hesitant offer similar assistance?

Most people pause before jumping into the water. When you do jump in, chances are you'll discover that "the water's fine."

6 Gathering

Purpose: To gain encouragement and ideas to find the people help you need; to share progress on Vocational Exploration Plans and practical parameters you want to change

Everyone bring:

    Examples of giving and receiving help from Segment 1
    Help Wanted pages from Segment 3
    Work from Segment 5

Vocational Exploration Plan from chapter 4, Segment 4

Practical parameters to change from chapter 3, Segment 3

WARM-UP (EVERYONE)
25 MINUTES

Tell some stories of times when you gave and/or received help that made a real difference. Add examples from people you know about if you have time.

REPORTS AND ENCOURAGEMENT (EVERYONE)
40 MINUTES

1. Each person speak about
   a. kinds of help he or she needs.
   b. candidates who could give it.
   c. calls made to acquire it.
   d. obstacles to selecting a person and asking for help.
2. Each person ask for encouragement or ideas to help him or her move forward.
3. Allow time for each person to record useful insights.

UPDATE (EVERYONE)
20 MINUTES

1. Reflect: Take a minute to review plans and actions related to your Vocational Exploration Plan and the practical parameters you want to change.
2. Share: Each person describe action taken on the Vocational Exploration Plan and on the practical parameters he or she wants to change.
3. Ask for assistance or affirmation to keep on track.

CLOSING (EVERYONE)
5 MINUTES

7 Build a Network

Entering her new consulting office, Kate glanced at the bare walls and functional furniture. "This space is dead. I've got to do something with it," she decided. Rather than display her diplomas, teaching certificate, and other emblems of achievement, she surrounded herself with photos—of her husband, a dear friend, her French teacher, the head of an organization she respected: those who had influenced and encouraged her. Imagine being supported in your work space by those who have had a hand in shaping you. It is a most impressive sight.

The newfound companions you have been thinking about join your existing community of allies and guides to form what might be called your personal network. These are the people who know you and care that you develop into the person you want to be. Rejoice in your widening group of resources and linkages. Value what you have, explore new possibilities, build your network.

Thinking about all the helpers he discovered, Jack said, "What comes to my mind is an image of a cobweb. I'm in the middle. Close by are Sally, my parents, and friends like Hal. A bit further out are friends at work and my new cabinetmaker friends. My banker and SCORE rep are there too. It's quite a comforting picture. And I thought I was quite alone with my dreams—except, of course, for Sally."

> **EXERCISE**
>
> Create a visual reminder of the helpers you've identified by drawing a cobweb with you in the middle. Place the names of your helpers at appropriate linking points.
>
> On your Summary Page for this chapter, list the names of key people you have identified who can support your present quest for meaningful work.
>
> Summarize what you've learned from this chapter. Note any questions you have.

Find NOURISHMENT for Your Whole Person

We can now understand that the fate of the soul is the fate of the social order, that if the spirit within us withers, so too will all the world we build about us. Theodore Roszak

6

1 Sustain the Soul

Picture yourself walking along a lonely beach. The sun tips the horizon, swathing the earth in a blaze of color. You are invigorated by a brisk wind brushing your face, soothed by the beat of the rolling waves. You walk along and feel at home in a friendly universe.

Scene Two. At a huge outdoor concert, you and hundreds of other fans listen and move to the performance of your favorite musical group. Applause and grateful voices pierce the air after every number. You are joyful, filled with emotion, as you and the rest of the concertgoers respond deeply to the music. You are part of a crowd of people uplifted by a common love.

Another scene. Your father has given you the old, worn table that once belonged to his father. You are in your basement surrounded by turpentine, stain remover, and rags. You lovingly restore the cherished table, exploring every crack, remembering where it once stood and how many times members of your family and their friends gathered around it for meals and celebrations. You feel connected with generations of your forebears and strengthened by their faithful living of life.

In each of these experiences, your life is nourished in ways that defy description. Words, in fact, may take something away from such experiences. You know they have happened. You savor their power. They have enriched your life and left you feeling restored, more whole, more at one with yourself and your world.

This "feeding of the whole person" is what is needed on a consistent basis if we are to discover and develop work from the heart. It is not that we lack convictions; most of us have strong beliefs about the contribution we would like our work to make. What is lacking is enough nourishment to sustain the depth of these convictions day in and day out as we try to express them through work.

As a Peace Corps volunteer in the Philippines, Ben felt pulled to devote his life to development work among impoverished people. When he read Dominique Lapierre's *City of Joy*, which describes the work of the Polish priest Stephan Kovalski among the desperately poor in Calcutta, Ben realized that he wanted something similar.

Recognizing, however, that he did not have the inward strength to do this work, he said, "I know that development work is going to take stamina and vision. But I'm not there yet. I care about people and want to do this kind of work, but I know I don't have the spiritual depth to sustain the long-term commitment I'd like to make. I need to learn how to refuel on a regular basis so I can weather the times when I will not see results or feel I'm doing anything worthwhile."

Ben recognized a basic truth. Just as plants and trees require regular nourishment from air, water, and sun, so we need to find what best feeds our whole being and brings alive the beliefs and values that mean most to us. When that special combination of body, mind, and spirit that is uniquely you is well fed, you are fully alive. You bring your best self to everything you do, including your work or search for work. Further, specific enrichment activities that are right for you can be sources of illumination or guidance for your work situation. A well-thought-out diet of nourishment also prevents burnout—that loss of energy, inspiration, and creativity that plagues so many of us at work.

All these are reasons to delve into the next step of the working from the heart process:

Find NOURISHMENT for your whole person.

To help us do this, Segment 1 highlights the importance of regular sustenance and invites us to revisit times in the past that were truly nourishing. Segment 2 explores the connection between creativity, nourishment, and meaningful work and then helps us tap into our own creativity. Segment 3 focuses on how to receive strength and guidance from transcendent sources. Segment 4 helps us identify a number of activities that could feed us now. Segment 5 encourages us to build some of these into our lives. And Segment 7 examines how to sustain a nourishing way of living and working.

To begin, build on what you already know about yourself. Consider those times in the past when you were fully alive and energized to bring your best to each endeavor. When Walt, a high school English teacher, did this, he remembered the beautiful impact of the first art film he had ever seen:

> I'll never forget the time I saw Ingmar Bergman's film *Seventh Seal*. The powerful photography haunted me. For months afterward, I pondered the meaning of life and death as presented in this wonderful movie.

Thinking about this experience heightened Walt's consciousness about how much films had enriched his life. He began remembering other films that had impressed him. Viewing them again freshened his appreciation. He began connecting this with his work as a teacher. Bringing examples from favorite films into the classroom fed his own enthusiasm and sparked student interest. In describing his work, Walt says, "I know of no more enjoyable way to convey the kinds of questions and values I want students to ponder than through exposing them to the fascinating art of film."

> **EXERCISE**
>
> Think back over your life. Remember three or four times when you felt that your whole being was nourished, lifted, invigorated—you choose the word. You may have had these experiences alone or with others. List them. Or make a drawing that gives expression to each of them.
>
> Select one to focus on now. Get back into it. Relive it. As you do so, depict with drawing and writing what you experienced. What were the circumstances? What did you do? How did you feel? What was inspiring or nurturing about it? Savor the reliving of this special moment.
>
> Ponder what you have drawn or written. Reflect on why the experience was important for you. In what ways were you nourished?
>
> As you proceed through this chapter with a consideration of the place of nourishment in your life, be alert, like Walt, to how this may relate to your worklife.

2 Thirty-Minute Workout for the Creative Spirit

The psychologist Rollo May defines creativity as "the process of bringing something new into being."[1] Whether we create a fresh solution to a business problem, a different way to play with the kids, or a sketch of a beautiful pine cone, the exercise of our creativity increases our capacity to engage constructively with life. Engaging our creativity releases energy for what we do and gives elegance to decisions we make.

"See what you can make with this," suggested Joan as she handed her friend Dave a lump of clay. "But I've never done anything like this before," Dave protested. "Don't worry about that," replied Joan. "Just fool around with it for a while, get quiet, begin to let it form itself."

Dave was part of a small group who had asked their art teacher friend, Joan, to help them try their hand at using clay and paints. A computer salesman in an understaffed company, most of his time is taken up with market analysis, costly decisions, and thorny installation problems.

Dave closed his eyes, settled himself, and played with the material, tossing it between his hands. It softened with his touch. He rolled it into a ball without any thought—then shaped the ball. "This is sorta fun," Dave mused. "I don't know if anything will come of it, but I sure feel relaxed." Gradually a form emerged. After a few minutes, Dave knew that he had finished what he wanted to make.

Setting his piece on a table, he gazed at it with admiration and exclaimed, "That's amazing! I never knew I could do something like this." Others in the room shared his wonder. The form had taken the shape of a nurturing woman holding a cherished object in her lap.

"That's beautiful!" said one of the others. "It reminds me of mothering."

Dave's wife added, "You know, it depicts how you are with me. You have a wonderful way of holding me and our life together in a calm and strong way." For Dave, this was an "aha!" experience—getting in touch with his artistic powers in a fresh and renewing way.

For Mary, a new way to express herself came through an altogether different medium. One day, while pushing her aging father in his wheelchair along the halls of the nursing home, she was surprised by his request: "Mary, I want to coast down the wheelchair ramp—give the chair a shove and let me go!"

Giving him a gentle push, Mary scurried to the bottom of the ramp to receive her father in his free-wheeling ride. She was elated by the exhilarated look on his face.

"That was great, Mary. Let's do it again!"

Suddenly, Mary was aware of how much movement, dance, sliding, skating, and rolling had meant to her father and how many playful hours they had once spent engaging in this nearly forgotten form of fun. Almost simultaneously, she realized how much she too loved movement and how much she missed having enough of it in her life. Like Dave's, her work life was full. As a college counselor, she found each day's schedule packed with students needing to discuss troubling situations.

As she planned her next vacation, Mary knew that movement was going to be a big part of it. Taking two weeks, she spent them in Arizona enrolled in a class led by a well-known eighty-year-old dancer. That same summer Mary turned sixty. "These wonderful weeks of dance were my birthday present to myself," she said, "it's been a long time since I've felt so deeply refreshed and alive."

What made these experiences so enlivening for Dave and Mary? A number of things. Both exercised aspects of their being that had not received much attention. In a very real sense, these parts of themselves came alive—Dave's artistic ability and Mary's love of movement. Taking time off from their usual routine, they both learned something new and had fun in the process. Their capacity to create was increased.

Dave and Mary also tapped their creativity. With spectator sports and television so prevalent, it is all too possible to lose touch with our own imaginative gifts—not because they are absent, but because they are not fully exercised.

Creativity expert Lois Robbins writes in her book *Waking Up in the Age of Creativity*, "While it is true that some talents seem to be inborn—witness the case of a precocious genius such as Mozart—there is now general agreement that we are all naturally endowed with creativity. But at some point in the growing-up process, it usually gets turned off or at least dampened with the result that as adults we use only about one-quarter of our capacity for creative work."[2]

When surveyed on what makes work meaningful, many people cite as first choice the desire to "exercise my ingenuity on the job." When we engage our creativity, we're able to be innovative, to begin "to think outside the box," to contribute insightfully to new situations.

EXERCISE

What follows is a smorgasbord of activities that cultivate, sustain, and replenish creativity. Taste a few of them. Savor the various sensations they evoke. Open new channels of illumination and sustenance for yourself.

Be present to nature. Many people take nature for granted. When you pay attention, however, newness leaps out at you. Here is Joseph Campbell's description of how this happened to him as a youngster:

> Going into the forest as a little boy, I can remember worshiping a tree, a great big old tree, thinking, "My, my, what you've known and been." I think this sense of the presence of creation is a basic mood of man. But we live now in a city. It's all stone and rock, manufactured by human hands. It's a different kind of world to

grow up in when you're out in the forest with the little chipmunks and the great owls. All these things are around you as presences, representing forces and powers and magical possibilities of life that are not yours and yet are all part of life, and that opens it out to you. Then you find it echoing in yourself, because you are nature. . . . It's a different way to live.[3]

Like Campbell, focus your attention on just one tree. Take time to admire it. Notice its trunk, branches, buds, leaves, or fruit. Imagine its roots. Express your appreciation for this wonderful gift of strength and beauty.

Commune with another person. To the question, "What activities are most nourishing to you?" a frequent response given by our seminar participants is, "Quality time with one other person."

A group of college friends met after thirty years. The talk started on the surface level until one friend said, "I'd like to tell you what has been going on with me since we last met." As the group listened to stories of a failed business, a new start, struggles with relationships, a search for grounding, they felt deep respect for their classmate. Another person followed suit. At the end of the evening, everyone felt refreshed. One remarked, "How wonderful it is to allow ourselves to get this close to one another."

Invite a friend or family member to spend some special time with you. Use that time to share your depths—your hopes, wishes, disappointments, places of suffering and joy, perhaps your search for the transcendent. After your time together, reflect and perhaps record how you were enhanced by this experience.

Write a poem. Arranging words artistically on a page highlights their significance. Choose phrases to express precisely how you feel. Distill the meaning you want to convey with each word chosen. That is poetry. There is no right way to create it.

What matters
is that
you feel your feelings deeply,
think your thoughts clearly,
choose your words carefully,
arrange them artfully.

Cultivate the outlaw part of yourself. In *Life Maps,* James Fowler and Sam Keen invite us to become outlaws. "The Outlaw stage begins with a crime, the killing of the old authorities."[4] Outlaws move beyond confining traps—traps that say, "I can't do anything different," or "It's always been like this."

One day Alice, a subway mechanic, felt unusually assaulted by the ugliness of her underground workplace. Out flowed a harsh poem full of unprintable language. Expressing her outrage in tangible form released pent-up energy. This freed her to beautify her work space. She cleaned her locker and put miniposters in it, began contemplating and expressing to her colleagues the strengths she saw in them, and then painted the whole shop in bright rainbow colors. Poetry unleashed her creativity. This freed up her outlaw self, which then went wild and crazy in transforming her workplace.

To become bigger, we need to break away from old understandings of ourselves and the world. Take a cue from Alice. Express the outlaw in yourself:

- Do one outrageous act.
- Speak out about something that's been bugging you.
- Give up the "duty" you planned this week and instead do something that challenges the status quo.

Which of the above smorgasbord of ideas appealed to you? Jot down your reactions to the activities you tried, the nourishment you received, and the relevance of these insights to your sense of yourself and meaningful work.

3
Be Open to Mystery and Transcendence

Alone in the woods, the Iroquois brave is on his vision quest. It is a time of transition. He leaves the tribe a boy and returns a man. Without food or shelter, confronted by his weakness, he must conjure up strength to survive. He seeks a totem—an element of nature—with which to identify. Caught in a furious storm, his body shakes with the roar of thunder. Then, suddenly, he experiences a radically different sensation. The thunder's energy and power becomes an inspiration, infusing him with confidence that he will find his way.

Seeking shelter under a rock, he falls asleep in peace. The next morning he locates edible roots that give him strength, enabling him to make his way back to the village. Walking triumphantly to the chief, he announces his name: Great Thunder.

What happened in this vision quest to change the frightened youngster into tall-standing Great Thunder? The answer lies in the realm of the indescribable. It involves a transfusion of energy and awareness from sources outside one's own consciousness, described by some as a mystical experience. It is what spiritual writers grope for as they picture a mystic moving from the stages of Purgation (emptying of false desires) to Illumination (having a vision of the good) to Union (being infused by the good). Marilyn Ferguson, in *The Aquarian Conspiracy*, attempts a description of the word *mystical*. "[It] derives from the Greek *mystos*, 'keeping silence.' Mystical experience reveals phenomena that are usually silent and inexplicable. This expanded consciousness, this whole-knowing, transcends our limited powers of description. Sensation, perception, and intuition seem to merge to create something that is none of these."[5]

The young brave far from the security of tribal life received illumination from the thunder. Then something much more startling occurred: he became one with the thunder. Its power was transferred to him, and he *became* Great Thunder.

However sublime, this experience is akin to something as simple as eating an apple. As you consume an apple, its energy is transferred to you. The apple is in you, and through the process of digestion, you receive energy from it.

Can we reproduce the conditions of the vision quest in our overcrowded lives, and more important, can we guarantee that an infusion of power and clarity will occur? We can arrange an infrequent but multi-day experience of solitude and openness like the vision quest. We can go apart on a daily basis to seek instruction, blessing, encouragement, and wisdom from sources outside ourselves. These practices may replicate the conditions of the vision quest, but results cannot be guaranteed. The very nature of the vision quest is to venture into the unknown. Yet if we open ourselves to receive energy, power, and guidance from contact with mystery and transcendence, there is an excellent chance that our intention will be rewarded.

Take a closer look at the Iroquois brave. He is part of a living spiritual tradition that espouses a particular spiritual path. The brave's vision quest marks his transition from seeker to initiate. To the quest for his new identity as an initiate, the brave brought an expectant spirit. He was looking for something and hopeful of finding it. His return marked his entrance as an initiate into a community of people dedicated to supporting each other in the path they have chosen. Whatever did or did not happen on the vision quest would be shared with those more experienced in the path, who would back his desire to grow as a faithful tribe member.

Ben, the Peace Corps volunteer we met in Segment 1, brought a similarly receptive attitude to the Zen monastery he entered on Mt. Baldy in California. "I want to learn to meditate," he said. "Being a lover of people, I can become much too distracted by their many demands. Through learning to meditate I hope to find my inner core and learn to live out of that."

Realizing this would be difficult for him to learn, he committed himself to a year in the monastery. "I want to postpone future vocational decisions until after this year, so that my thinking can be informed by my meditation practice," he said.

A year after his monastic experience, Ben married and entered graduate school. He had to adapt what he learned on Mt. Baldy to his new circumstances. Each day he sets aside a time for meditation. Periodic visits to the local Zen center to meditate with others encourages his devotion.

Like the young Iroquois and Ben, we too can seek instruction, blessing, encouragement, and wisdom from sources outside ourselves. As we do this, there is an excellent chance that the receptivity we bring to it will bear fruit.

EXERCISE

1. Reflect in writing on these questions: Is there a living spiritual tradition that draws you? What is it? What do you know of the spiritual path it espouses? How would you like to relate to this path? As an inquirer to learn more about it? As a seeker considering whether you wish to take this path? Or as an initiate committed to embarking on it? What do you need in order to learn the ways of this particular path?

2. If you wish, arrange your own "mini-vision quest." Figure a way that suits you or select one or both of the following activities. Allow at least forty-five minutes for each of these activities.

- Withdraw from usual activity. Move to a favorite spot. This may be inside or outdoors. If you are in your own home, consider playing music you find particularly moving. Relax, and let it fill you with its power. Open to it as completely as possible. Let it fill your whole being. Receive what it has to offer you. If you are in another indoor location or outdoors, soak up the atmosphere. Be fully present to where you are.

Then consider your life at this juncture and the contribution you would like to offer others. Ask for a "life image," word, or sense of transcendent power. Be receptive and attentive, open to what happens.

When you have finished, rest a few minutes and absorb what has occurred. Record what you wish to remember. (It is important to engage in this activity without specific expectations. A sense of "oughtness" may block glimpses of what may be given. Whatever happens, value your openness to new experience. You may have to repeat this activity several times before you experience power from outside yourself.)

- Create a sacred space where you can be particularly centered and open to receiving spiritual gifts from outside yourself. Furnish it with reminders of that which is holy. This may be as simple as a central burning candle on the dining room table or a notebook where you place beautiful photos or pieces of wisdom that speak to you. Then spend a period of time there. Bring a central question that concerns you. Ask it and be open to what occurs. Or simply bring yourself for a time of being, not doing, in the presence of that which is greater than yourself. Rest in the presence of the holy.

4. Find What Works for You

Always an avid reader, Bill would sink into his favorite chair with a good book after returning home from his law firm. This was his way of recharging. But lately the written word has lost its appeal. "I feel flooded with words," he says. "Junk mail, newspapers, speeches, articles—words, spoken and written. I'm sick of verbiage. I'm beginning to crave nonverbal forms of replenishment."

Bill has started walking each day. He's appreciating the seasonal changes. This has triggered an interest in gardening. He is now outside in all kinds of weather. One thing has led to another. "I didn't know what I was missing," he says. Living closer to nature's cycles has brought a calm and refreshment he had not expected. Still a book lover, Bill now reads more selectively, leaving time to savor what he takes in. As he has learned to feed both physical and mental parts of himself, Bill feels more alive.

It takes some experimentation for each of us to come up with a combination of activities that not only nourish our whole being but also can be readily included in our routine. As you consider how to do this, here are some tips to keep in mind:

Build contrast into the ways you replenish your spirit. Consider both being and doing, engagement and retreat, solitude and community, verbal and nonverbal experience, serious commitment and time for playing hooky.

Think about your need for both roots and wings as you choose ways to nourish the deepest parts of yourself. In a college alumni magazine, a reader wrote, "I have learned that I want to give my children roots and wings—we all need a tie to the traditional and a lift toward the new."

Sarah routinely and regularly reads a bit of sacred writing from one of the great religious traditions of the world. "This grounds me in ancient wisdom," she says. "In addition to that, I also love to read current books that are pushing and integrating the frontiers of knowledge."

Feed all parts of yourself—body, mind, and spirit. The words of a Catholic priest, Thomas Ryan, in his book *Wellness, Spirituality, and Sports,* are instructive:

> The central concern of spirituality is fullness of life. Since the only life we know is earthly and sensual, it follows that this is the stuff of our spirituality. Hence, even such things as running and jumping and skiing and swimming can become part of our language with God. The challenge of any spirituality is to integrate all the aspects of life in our engagement with the world. We arrive at wholeness by using to the fullest the stuff of our human experience, rather than by denying or diminishing it or seeing it as outside the pale of our relationship with God.[6]

One part—body, mind, or spirit—might claim your attention for now. But over time give each generous sustenance to keep vital.

Combine receiving the insight, energy, and techniques of others with conceiving your own ideas, images, and practices. At galleries, Alan drinks in the art of the masters, but at home he draws or paints images that come from within himself. Reading the wisdom of others can be complemented by writing your own insights gained through experience.

The following chart highlights the contrast between receiving and conceiving. Read the parallel lines in each column and savor the contrast.

Receiving	*Conceiving*
• reading the thoughts of others	• writing your own thoughts
• thinking about the experiences of the day	• sharing experiences or stories of the day with family or friends
• learning the wisdom of the ages	• recording personal wisdom gained through own experience
• viewing other people's art, dance, drama	• creating your own art, dance, drama
• watching sports	• participating in sports
• seeing others' gardens	• making your own garden

Trust your own judgment as to what works for you. Allow your gut responses to lead you to fresh experiences.

Some people require contrast between what they do at work and how they find replenishment. Ted holds a highly interactive, fast-moving management job during the week. On weekends, he likes to wander by himself in the countryside, explore old architecture, and perhaps pick up an item for his collection of nineteenth-century toys. This enables him to be more centered when he returns to work.

Meg is different. A state leader in wildflower preservation, she likes nothing better in her spare time than to nurture her interest in plants. On vacations she visits great gardens. Ecology field trips offer fresh insight. And digging in her own garden also brings a glow of rejuvenation.

EXERCISE

You've just read about a variety of nourishing experiences that mean something to others. What about yourself? For what does your soul hunger? What do your body, your mind, and your spirit need to operate in top condition? What kinds of activities make you feel truly alive? List several. Then reread this segment, paying particular attention to the tips.

Do these trigger other activities to add to your list? Approach this as a brainstorming exercise.

- How am I incorporating this experience into my life now?
- How is it affecting me?
- How would I like to incorporate it in the future?

5 Build Nourishment into Each Day

It is one thing to have an occasional walk in a beautiful forest or a night at the theater absorbing a well-crafted play. It is quite another to build into your life regular, intentional periods of nourishment that provide ongoing energy and guidance needed to live life fully and to work more creatively. This we must do to operate at full capacity.

People who want to keep in good physical shape know the importance of regular physical exercise. The way they go about incorporating it into their lives varies. Judy is a planner. She schedules jogging into her day rain or shine. Not a day passes without spending at least one hour in this refreshing activity.

Nick, equally enthusiastic about physical conditioning, is an in-the-moment sort of person. In his garage are a bike, some skis, a tennis racket, and garden tools. Outside is a canoe. Everything is at hand. On a given day, depending on the weather and his other commitments, he can create the kind of physical conditioning that is right for that day. Surrounding himself with possibilities, he is committed to choosing some physical activity each day. That works well for him.

Like Judy or Nick, we must all include physical activity in our lives. Mental and spiritual food are crucial as well. To create and sustain a nourishing lifestyle, it is helpful to give and receive support from someone equally committed to this. This support may involve something as simple as discussing the question, "How are you doing?" during a weekly phone call or lunch date. Or it may entail meeting with like-minded people who choose certain practices in common and provide group energy to do them. This is what Mark does related to his desire to maintain a healthy diet.

"I know I should eat right," he says. What helps me in this intention is regular attendance at Weight Watchers. When asked what makes the program work for him, he replied, "Three things. Support, check-ins, and pep talks. I go with a friend who's also committed to keeping fit. Each time we attend, our weight is checked. That way we keep on track. And the pep talks give excellent ideas on healthy eating."

EXERCISE

1. Are you a planner or an in-the-moment person? Select the activity that suits you best from the two here.

- **For planners.** Look over the work you have done for this chapter. Review the life-sustaining experiences you have valued in the past and new ideas that have come to you. Which of these would you like to schedule regularly into your life? Choose four.

    With colored markers or pens, draw these in your notebook as the "four posts" that will support a flourishing lifestyle. Include a statement about how frequently you will engage in these. Call this your Nourishment Plan and bring it to share during the Gathering session.

- **For in-the-moment people.** Look over what you have done for this chapter. Choose three categories of experience that will most enhance the next period of your life. Create spaces in your home where you can place the materials/equipment necessary for these activities—for example, a shelf of art materials in your living room, a bike in your garage. Create pockets of space in your week that are reserved for this refreshment. During those times, engage in the activity that will most rejuvenate you at that moment.

    Describe or draw these arrangements you have made. Call this your Marketplace of Possibilities. Bring it to the Gathering session.

2. Consider the benefits of having a "buddy" with whom to share your commitment to nourishing your whole person. Who could serve in this capacity?

6 Gathering

Purpose: To encourage your commitment to inner nourishment by sharing and learning from others

Leaders bring: Newsprint, magic markers

Everyone bring:

> List of nourishing experiences from Segment 1
>
> Nourishment Plan or Marketplace of Possibilities from Segment 5

WARM-UP (EVERYONE)
20 MINUTES

1. Describe one experience of inner sustenance from your past that has been particularly good (from Segment 1).
2. What new practice have you tried or would you like to try for refreshment?

FEEDBACK AND ENCOURAGEMENT (IN FOURS)
45 MINUTES

1. Share your Nourishment Plan or Marketplace of Possibilities. Ask for feedback based on the following questions (thirty minutes):
   a. Is it realistic?
   b. Is it balanced?
   c. Is it energizing?
2. Discuss how the inner nourishment you build into your life relates to the work you do (fifteen minutes).

PLAN FOR SUPPORT (IN TWOS)
5 MINUTES

Speak about the kind of support you need to keep your commitment to a nourishing lifestyle. Discuss how you can provide for this.

ENCOURAGEMENT HUDDLE (EVERYONE)
15 MINUTES

Put some newsprint on the floor with lots of markers. Huddle around and write the most encouraging words you can think of, words that will send you off in good spirits to live more fully this week. Share the words. Perhaps illustrate with a drawing or two.

CLOSING (EVERYONE)
5 MINUTES

7 Keep Energy Flowing

You have decided to give yourself the kind of nourishment you need. As you pay attention to this need, you will taste the benefits of your commitment.

Give yourself time to allow these new practices to work. It is said that to establish a new habit requires six months or fifty repetitions. Daily practice of scales on the piano yields the hand strength and position to produce beautiful music. So it is with the kinds of "spiritual practice" we have been describing.

Don't let your nourishment practices go stale. Ask yourself, Is my routine "life-giving"? Does it "work"? Is there enough freshness as well as stability? Be honest with yourself. What works well at one time may be deadly at another. Although we have touched on the sacred in what we've been describing, there are no sacred cows. Experiment. Find what most enlivens and feeds you.

When you sense that you are ready for change in what you have been doing, it may be that, like Bill, whose reading no longer enlivened him, you will be ready to give attention to another dimension of your life. To expand your thinking, consider the research carried out by business consultant Ann McGee-Cooper. She concludes that there are twelve "key life factors" that influence the amount of energy we bring to our work.[7] These are included in an assessment tool created by McGee-Cooper and are to be found in appendix D. Use this tool to remind you of factors in your life that may require attention.

> **EXERCISE**
>
> Review your Nourishment Plan or Marketplace of Possibilities from Segment 5. Modify what you came up with, if that seems indicated. Then commit yourself to carrying it out.
>
> Choose something that you can carry in your pocket or purse as a symbol of what nourishes you. This might be a shell representing freedom or a stone that calls you to integrity. As you touch your object throughout the day, take a moment to absorb the sustenance it represents. Allow it to influence how you go about your work.
>
> If you have chosen a nourishment "buddy," keep that person's name and phone number in a visible place. Let it remind you of your shared commitment.
>
> On the Summary Page for this chapter, record the Nourishment Plan or Marketplace of Possibilities you are committed to for the next period of time. Finally, summarize your learnings from this chapter. What questions emerge that need attention?

Contribute to an Effective WORK COMMUNITY

We hunger for community in the workplace and are a great deal more productive when we find it. To feed this hunger... is to harness energy and productivity beyond imagining.
Marvin R. Weisbord

Together We Can Do Better

The Madeira School, an independent high school for young women, sits perched on a cliff high above the Potomac River. Far below, one's eye is held by the boiling rapids at Difficult Run. Since 1906, Madeira has been an educational leader, known for its active, interested faculty and lively, intelligent student body. It was without hesitation that we accepted the school's invitation to help out with a pre-semester orientation for its student leaders.

When the appointed day came, we stood before the young women and asked simply, "What type of school do you want to create this year?" With little prompting, their thoughts on the subject tumbled out, filling the room with a spirit of hope. Here is how they summarized their thinking: "In our school we want *unity* but also respect for *individual diversity*. We want Madeira to be a place where we can have *pride* in ourselves, our work, and our school."

In an hour's time, these teenagers pinned down the characteristics that would make Madeira School an effective work community for them. Intuitively, they knew a basic truth: No matter how motivated an individual is to do an excellent job, if the work community is not organized to support that motivation, the worker becomes less creative, more dispirited, and ultimately less productive. Conversely, *when the work community supports our desire to do our best, we are more creative, more energetic, more effective.*

When the workplace supports our best work, employees are fairly paid, a good spirit prevails among the staff, the work itself is worthwhile. People labor hard and happily, learn much, and grow. They are part of a team dedicated to producing excellent work. They are a community, an assemblage of people bound together by common goals and a common organization. This enables them to accomplish more than they thought they could.

In nonsupportive workplaces, performance is not fairly evaluated, compensation is inadequate, the work space itself is unattractive or inefficient.

In good situations, you labor with ease, and your product is a thing of quality. In bad ones, you chafe and buck and find yourself longing for a change.

This chapter focuses on a key step:

Contribute to an effective WORK COMMUNITY.

To contribute involves offering your best work no matter what conditions prevail in your workplace. It also includes identifying where change is needed and doing your part to help that happen.

"Who, me?" you say. "Who am I to call for a change in policy or stand up to an unreasonable boss?" Yes, you! A journey of a thousand miles begins with a single step. That step could be yours. There is plenty you can do as an individual to make your workplace hum! You can increase your ability to do top-notch work and you can make improvements alone, with others, and with or without your boss.

This chapter's purpose is to raise issues and incite action. Segment 1 focuses on the importance of a supportive workplace. In Segment 2, characteristics of a good work environment are described, and you are invited to use these to evaluate your own workplace or those you visit in your search for work. Segment 3 explores the variety of change-making actions available to you as you consider how you can foster greater workplace effectiveness. This prepares you for Segment 4, which describes steps for initiating change as well as workplace arenas affected by change. Segment 5 explores changes we can make in ourselves that make us more effective contributors. Segment 7 looks at how the concept of the workplace as a community creates, in itself, a climate for change. We also look at the timing for effective change.

> **EXERCISE**
>
> Think of three times when a community (not necessarily your workplace) you belonged to helped you do something that you had always wanted to do. Describe these in your notebook. Recall some of the elements that served as catalysts.

2 "A Great Place to Work"— Ideal and Reality

On a hunt for America's "superlative employers," labor and business reporter Robert Levering interviewed employees and managers to learn what makes a company a truly wonderful place to work. His findings are recorded in *A Great Place to Work*.[1] John Naisbitt and Patricia Aburdene, in *Re-inventing the Corporation*, describe innovations that top-notch companies undertake to respond to today's trends.[2] MIT professor Peter M. Senge, in *The Fifth Discipline*, shows how to build a learning organization that is "continually expanding its capacity to create its future."[3]

Each of these thinkers names qualities that comprise effective work communities. These we have grouped under the key words in the "work from the heart" steps. As you read them, note those that are particularly important to you. The insights and examples offered by these thinkers relate to companies but also can be adapted to other organizations such as schools and community groups.

GIFTS

Work from the heart involves using our gifts to do something we enjoy and believe in. The supportive workplace helps us do precisely that.

Naisbitt and Aburdene say that more people than ever want work that is both fulfilling and enjoyable. This satisfaction occurs when we are encouraged to use our creativity in designing our work, when we are involved in decision making, when results are rewarded and quality performance is emphasized, when we are given room to challenge the status quo and offer alternatives.

MEANING

Work from the heart incorporates ideals, vision, and values most important to us. The effective work community has a sense of purpose clearly articulated, subject to review, and supported by each worker. Naisbitt and Aburdene write, "Only a company with a real mission or sense of purpose that comes out of an intuitive or spiritual dimension will capture people's hearts. And you must have people's hearts to inspire the hard work required to realize a vision."[4]

Naisbitt and Aburdene describe vision as "the link between dream and action."[5] When we envision the future we want to create, they say, we can more easily achieve our goal. When our personal mission coincides with our organization's vision, a sense of alignment and momentum gives purpose to the work we do.

When our organization's purpose, program, and products contribute to the well-being of society, our particular work fosters the greater good. We also appreciate seeing tangible expressions of social responsibility, such as corporate donations to service organizations in which employees participate.

PARAMETERS

Work from the heart includes taking into account our practical parameters. The effective workplace offers resources to help us do that. For example, companies organize child care facilities, offer backup help for ill employees, and provide wellness programs to keep people in top physical and emotional condition.

Organizations that give attention to people's practical concerns outside work draw more committed participation.

VOCATIONAL DREAMS

Working from the heart means moving toward the realization of our vocational aspirations, that work which we see as truly worth doing. Effective work communities encourage us to do research, undergo training, and seek out broadening experiences that will help us grow vocationally and personally.

An important question for many people who go to work in an organization is, What will I learn? Peter Senge uses the term "personal mastery" to describe the "discipline of personal growth and learning." According to Senge, "People with high levels of personal mastery are continually expanding their ability to create the results in life they truly seek. From their quest for continual learning comes the spirit of the learning organization."[6]

PEOPLE

Work from the heart involves giving and receiving personal support along the way. Supportive workplaces see that the best response to the question, "Who is there for me?" is, *"We all are!"*

In today's best-run organizations, top-down management is complemented by collegial structures that promote the feeling, "We are all in this together." Teamwork, self-management, small autonomous working groups, and open communication foster a "we" approach to getting things done rather than an "us against them" scenario.

NOURISHMENT

Work from the heart is sustained by a nourishing lifestyle. The supportive workplace provides opportunities for all parts of us—body, mind, and spirit—to be fed.

Professional workshops offer a change of scene, opportunity for new learning and study, contact with colleagues, and often travel—all of which give people fresh energy and insight into their work. Plants and trees, art, colorful decor, and creative architecture contribute an ambiance that lifts people's spirits and encourages them to do high-quality work. Exercise equipment available for those who want to work out signals a company's commitment to wellness.

As you think of how this sampling of effective workplace characteristics applies to your own situation, there are two steps to take.

First, form a clear picture of the workplace characteristics that are most important to you now. In looking for a job in city management, Henry, whom you first met in Chapter 4, knew what he wanted in his work environment: "I want to work with people I enjoy. That will be one of the first things I'll look for when I interview. Also I'd like to have a job that doesn't keep me at a desk all day long. I'll be looking to see how much those who interview me expect me to be in the office and how much they want me to be 'out and about' the town. Because I'm single, money isn't as important to me as it is to some people."

Second, assess what is positive about your workplace, what needs changing, what is unlikely to change. (If you are searching, consider a place you have visited.)

"How do you like your new job?" Pam was asked three months after starting as a recreation therapist at a rehabilitation hospital. She replied:

> The staff is good. The facility is fine—we have all the equipment we need. I like my patients and my particular work. But two things bother me. I really don't like my supervisor's personality. We just don't click. The other thing is more specific. My supervisor put off my first evaluation until after I had been here for three months. Then when we did meet, there was not much time. I had saved up a bunch of questions and just didn't get a chance to ask them. I would like more frequent conversations with my supervisor.

Pam identified some things she appreciates about her job and two things she does not like. The first one, her boss's personality, is unlikely to change. The other, too few meetings with her supervisor, might change.

Henry and Pam know that any one workplace can't be ideal, but they are clear about what matters most to them. Henry knows what he is looking for. Pam has focused on what she appreciates and what she can or cannot change in her work environment.

EXERCISE

1. List one or two workplace characteristics that are important to you now. Describe this in words or create an art piece with line and color depicting why these are important. Use what you have just read as a stimulus for your own thinking.

2. Focus on where you work or study or, if you are searching for work, a workplace you have recently visited. List in writing three things about this workplace that lift you up and three that get you down. For the three that get you down, identify which might change and which are unlikely to change.

3 Surface the Possibilities for Change

You've identified workplace characteristics you care about. You've also looked at one workplace and identified qualities that lift you up and those that pull you down. Regarding those that give you a headache, you've decided which might change and which are unlikely to change. Given this awareness, how can you contribute to an effective work community?

Start with affirming the good you see—the glass *is* half full. Spontaneous unexpected appreciation adds a wonderful spirit to anyone's day. It is all too easy to gripe about the bad and take the good for granted. Yet, affirming the positive often increases its influence. When a local college dean sent a questionnaire to all staff asking about needs for a child care facility on campus, many respondents not only filled out the form but added a note of thanks to the administrator for caring about their family needs. The dean was so delighted that she doubled her commitment to providing good child care for the staff.

Regarding characteristics that cause you to groan, separate what could change from what is unlikely to change. Then focus on where you might make a difference. There are many more possibilities to initiate change than most of us think.

Picture yourself somewhere in the middle of an organization that is traditionally structured with a chain of command. In what directions could you initiate change? You can change what's below you (that might be the easiest), what's around you (a bit more difficult), and sometimes what's above you (the most challenging).

Now consider the *actions of change*. Suppose you want to see your company begin to recycle. Here are five change-making actions you could use.

1. **Model** the desired change.
   You could collect the recyclable items you produce and then take them yourself to a recycling center. People below, around, and above you might notice your efforts and be inspired to do the same.
2. Informally **stimulate** the desired change.
   In casual conversation, you could talk about the benefits of recycling and encourage others to recycle. Again, this could happen with superiors, subordinates, and peers.
3. **Request** the desired change.
   You could ask the company to initiate a recycling program. That would involve dealing with people above you. It might also be possible to suggest that peers and subordinates recycle even though it's not yet company policy.
4. **Plan** the desired change.
   You could start a recycling committee that would research and design a recycling program.
5. **Mandate** the desired change.
   This action is possible with those directly responsible to you.

The grid that follows charts the *direction of change* related to *change-making actions*. The checkmarked actions are possible for you to use to initiate change, given your midlevel position in the organization. The X-marked ones are not. Notice that out of fifteen change-making actions, you can carry out thirteen. That's a lot of change-making power!

If appropriate, bring alive the truth of this grid by identifying a needed change in your organization. Consider whether this change can best be effected alone or with others. If you need the help of others, brainstorm with colleagues specific actions people at different levels could take to help it happen.

As a newly hired manager of a retail grocery store, Larry proposed to the owners a change in company policy that would encourage hiring refugees ambitious for a fresh start. But the owners resisted. For the time being, Larry settled for changing those things for which he alone was responsible:

Change-Making Opportunities I Have at Work (✓ = can do; x = cannot do)			
CHANGE-MAKING ACTIONS	DIRECTION OF CHANGE		
	Below	Around	Above
MODEL desired change	✓	✓	✓
STIMULATE desired change	✓	✓	✓
REQUEST desired change	✓	✓	✓
PLAN desired change	✓	✓	✓
MANDATE desired change	✓	x	x

organizing a well-run store, being resourceful and accessible to customers and employees, and setting a tone of easygoing informality by his warm, caring approach.

Acting together to enrich their work, State Department employees decided they wanted to rub elbows with key decision makers and international thinkers. They instituted the Brown Bag Forum, a weekly lunch open to all State Department personnel, where well-known speakers articulate their policy views and open the floor to vigorous challenge and discussion.

EXERCISES

1. Pick out a handful of people where you work whose actions have created a brighter, better, more empowering workplace. Think of a creative way to say, "Thanks, I appreciate what you do." Or if you are still in

search of work, note three workplace situations where an "angel's" hand is in evidence—where good work is done with an upbeat spirit. How would you thank the "angel" if you worked there?

2. Select one significant but do-able change you would like to see happen in your workplace. List that in your notebook. Note whether this change is something to be done alone or with others. What change-making actions seem appropriate? Keep in mind what you've written as you read Segment 4, which offers more tools for initiating change.

The Powerful Act of Making Change

"If I listed everything I'd change at work, it would rival Plato's collected works in length," lamented Arnold, an assistant professor of philosophy at a major university. "The status quo seems a monolith against which I am impotent. What can I do?"

Change is the process of directing an already moving chain of events. These five steps are usually involved:

- Picture where you want to go
- Consider alternative ways to get there
- Choose which steps to take
- Anticipate and deal effectively with obstacles
- Make midcourse corrections when circumstances change or obstacles cannot be overcome

It is as if you were sailing at sea. Even if you sat perfectly still, making not a move to control the vessel, you would be moving. To reach a destination, you need to spot your objective—a small island perhaps—trim the sails, and then continually make fine adjustments in your rudder and sail positions to keep on course.

In the workplace, an accurate, inspiring picture of the change you envision is the first step toward greater effectiveness. When Arnold thought about it, he realized he was bogged down by a jumble of complaints that didn't really lead toward change. That's not uncommon. Complaints have a way of sticking to each other to form a *giant congealed unmanageable mess!* Arnold knew he could do something, maybe not solve all the problems himself, but at least contribute to solutions. But where to begin, especially when his colleagues seemed too busy to get involved? To get these concerns out of his system, he jotted down all his complaints on paper. That made him feel a bit better. Then he sorted them into categories: "urgent," "important," "later." Top on his list of "urgents" was his black mood. He framed this question, What one change would really lift my spirits and help me believe that my work matters? After some thought, this is what he came up with: "We teach philosophy to students but never talk about it among ourselves as faculty. I'd like to converse with colleagues about what currently excites us in philosophy, how it impacts our lives, and what difference it makes in the world."

Once Arnold had envisioned a desired change, he began to think of options. Several emerged. He could begin talking with department colleagues about his desire for more intellectual stimulation. He could then gather those interested to brainstorm ways to bring this about. If no one at work responded to his ideas, he could consider gathering philosophy professionals outside the department. Whatever path Arnold chooses, change has begun.

So far, we have focused, as Arnold did, on changing what first comes to your mind as mattering most to you. For a broader view of ways to contribute to an effective workplace, consider with colleagues the variety of *arenas for change,* all beginning with the letter *P!* This is not an exhaustive list but an easily remembered beginning.

> **Purpose**—How can we join informally or officially in defining or refining mission?
>
> **Policy and procedure**—How can we create structures that foster each person's best work?
>
> **Program or product**—How can we add to the quality and value of how and what we produce?
>
> **Personal**—What arrangements matter most to us related to time, leave, training? How can we support each other personally at work?
>
> **Physical**—How can we create a more healthy environment in which to work?

To begin, focus on change that is do-able and likely to be successful. That small success will ready you for more challenging change.

> **EXERCISE**
>
> Related to the do-able change you selected in Segment 3, create a Workplace Change Plan. Be specific about
>
> - The change you envision
> - Obstacles you expect and strategies to meet them
> - Steps you will take alone or with others toward that change
>
> Take as many of the steps as possible before the Gathering.
>
> If you are looking for work, come to the Gathering with any ideas you have about helping change happen in the workplace or ideas you have implemented in past situations. Jot them down now for ready reference.

5. Trump Card for Transformation — Change Yourself

So far our discussion has focused on initiating change in the workplace. Now we focus on ourselves—how we might change in order to be more effective contributors at work. Whether your workplace welcomes change or not, how you come to the workplace makes a huge difference in the amount of satisfaction you receive.

Motivational expert Dr. Ross West discovered research that reveals a surprising fact: "What makes people happy in their jobs is *not* simply the reverse of what makes them unhappy."[7] How does this principle work out in practice?

Here are the kinds of things that make people dissatisfied with their jobs:

- Supervision
- Company policy
- Working conditions
- Interpersonal relations
- Salary
- Status
- Job security
- Events in one's life

If all these matters were well taken care of, an individual would not necessarily be happy. The person would simply not be unhappy, notes Dr. West.[8] A pretty "neutral," blah state!

The factors that workers themselves claim bring job satisfaction include these:

- Achievement
- Recognition for achievement
- The work itself
- Responsibility
- Advancement
- Possibility for growth

These are all matters we ourselves can do something about! Sure, it's great to get positive feedback from colleagues and supervisors, but recognize how much you can do for yourself in these areas. Take a look.

- **Achievement.** To increase your sense of accomplishment on the job, be proactive. Think through the kinds of achievements you would like to realize in a given time period. Then track how you are doing related to those objectives. Finally, record accomplishments you feel really good about. This will strengthen your sense of achievement on the job. You'll also have an accurate record for evaluation time and for résumé writing.

- **Recognition for achievement.** Recognize and record the positive feedback you receive. That points to strengths that you want to keep in your awareness. It also may be appropriate to ask clients who are appreciative of your services to write a note of thanks to you or your organization. That kind of feedback does not go unnoticed.

- **The work itself.** Related to the work you do, master the basics and learn new skills. Top quality work makes you feel proud. That is a prime source of meaning and satisfaction.

- **Responsibility and advancement.** Prepare for this by mastering your present job and acquiring the skills it takes to do higher-level work. Consider also whether you want that. The next level up the career ladder might lead to misery if it requires you to use skills you don't have or do not like to use.

- **Possibility for growth.** Be intentional about learning on and off the job. Each experience, criticism, and training opportunity is a chance to grow and to learn new things.

EXERCISES

1. Identify one thing you could do today or tomorrow to bring more competence and "can do" spirit to your work. Then go for it! In your notebook, record what you did and the result.

2. Review the components of your job—what you are expected to do and what you actually accomplish. Think about one achievement at work that you really enjoyed. Which of your strengths were active in that achievement? Identify one way to build on that strength or use it again. Ross West notes, "The payoff for building on your strengths is greater than the payoff for getting a little better at the things you're weak in" because you may be able to become more expert in the area of your strengths and increase your enjoyment as well.[9]

3. Write the achievement you enjoyed on a colorful 3 x 5 card. Dash out to the stationery store and buy a flashy new card box. Slip your card in it. That will start one of the most valuable collections you'll ever have—your Achievement Box. Don't leave it with just one card. Make a habit of writing up enjoyable achievements and filling your box. Include specific details on each achievement: where it happened, with whom, and the results.

4. Think of people who do the quality and kind of work you really want to do. Learn about them through conversation or reading (if they are not known to you personally). Glean from them the developments in the field that seem most promising. Soak up these people's wisdom and make it part of your own.

Address these questions suggested by Ross West: What do they know that I don't know? What do they do well that I have some abilities in myself, that I could develop further?[10]

6 Gathering

Purpose: To share how workplace environments support work from the heart; to consider how you can help realize these conditions in your workplace or look for them in a place of future employment

Leaders bring: Newsprint, magic markers

Everyone bring: Your written work from Segments 1, 2, 3, 4, and 5

WARM-UP (EVERYONE)
15 MINUTES

1. Popcorn ways in which work environments you know have either enabled or stifled work from the heart (refer to the work you did for Segment 1).
2. Tell a few stories about pats on the back you have given or are thinking about giving (refer to the work you did for Segment 3).

ENCOURAGEMENT (THREES)
40 MINUTES

WHAT MATTERS MOST

1. Each person share their art piece or list of work characteristics that matter to him or her (Segment 2).
2. Regarding your present or imagined workplace, speak about what is positive, what needs changing, and what is unlikely to change (Segment 2).

HOW CAN I MAKE A DIFFERENCE?

1. Set up a role play. The first person reads their Workplace Change Plan. Two listeners act as the person's work colleagues, interested in joining the plan and carrying it out. The listeners give responses to the plan for change, questioning and challenging it in useful ways.
2. Together help each other in naming a desirable next step.
3. Then give each listener a turn to share their plan in a similar role play.

EXPERIENCE AND AFFIRMATION (EVERYONE)
30 MINUTES

1. Share possibilities and obstacles related to enabling change:

   - experiences when you have seen change happen in the workplace and the steps that were involved
   - experiences when you have seen change thwarted in the workplace and possible alternative ways the situation(s) could have been handled

2. Popcorn (and put on newsprint if you wish) words and phrases that will encourage you to bring about change in the workplace, either now or in the future.

CLOSING (EVERYONE)
5 MINUTES

7 Community—The Climate for Change

Max DePree has spent a lifetime creating the widely acclaimed Herman Miller furniture company in Zeeland, Michigan. He believes a well-run workplace functions as a community continually open to change and increased effectiveness. In his two books on leadership, *Leadership Is an Art* and *Leadership Jazz,* he describes lessons he and his colleagues have learned from long years of building the company.[11]

An effective workplace, according to DePree, involves a dynamic interplay between leader and employees much akin to the interaction that goes on among jazz musicians. He writes,

Creative work needs the ethos of jazz. . . . A leader will pick the tune, set the tempo, and start the music, define a "style." After that, it's up to the band to be disciplined and free, wild and restrained—leaders and

followers, focused and wide-ranging, playing the music for the audience and accountable to the requirements of the band. Jazz-band leaders know how to integrate the "voices" in the band without diminishing their uniqueness. The individuals in the band are expected to play solo *and* together. What a wonderful way to think of a vital and productive organization![12]

People in such an organization are bound together not simply by contract but by covenant. Contractual relationships, writes DePree, "cover such things as expectations, benefits, incentive opportunities, constraints, timetables, etc. These are all a part of our normal life and need to be there."[13]

More is needed, according to DePree, and that is the realm of covenant:

A covenantal relationship rests on shared commitment to ideas, to issues, to values, to goals and to management processes. Words such as love, warmth, personal chemistry are certainly pertinent. Covenantal relationships are open to influence. They fill deep needs, and they enable work to have meaning and to be fulfilling. Covenantal relationships reflect unity and grace and poise. They are an expression of the sacred nature of relationships.

Covenantal relationships enable corporations to be hospitable to the unusual person and to unusual ideas. Covenantal relationships tolerate risk and forgive errors.[14]

DePree believes that the best management process for today's environment is participative management based on covenantal relationships, everyone helping everyone else. This means "polishing gifts," making room for each person's gifts to be used, becoming "frantic learners," enabling one another to reach full potential and to "do something to make the world more beautiful."[15]

It also requires what DePree calls "lavish communication."[16] This includes questioning, clarifying, scrutinizing, and challenging what happens not only in work but also in relationships.

An organization that sees itself as a learning, caring, and producing community expects and adapts to constant change. When any part of such an organization is weak, the whole suffers. What is needed is a holistic remedy involving many parts of the organization, including individuals, structures, climate. The questions for improving the workplace then become not only, How can I do better? but also, What structural or systemic changes would enable us all to do our best?

As we see ourselves as people who foster workplace innovation and improvement, it is useful to understand what potential there is for change or action in our organization. To determine this, consultant Marvin Weisbord asks three questions:

1. Is there a leader willing to take risks for change?
2. Is there a business opportunity crying to be met?
3. Are there people energized to do things differently?[17]

Lucky is the organization that has all three in place. If yours does, the chances are that your suggestions for change and increased effectiveness are likely to be welcomed.

But if the time does not seem right for change, take heart—things do not remain static. Bosses change; companies are reorganized; people move on.

You have a backpack full of useful items to take out when you need them and when the time is right. You've set up one-half of the equation for change. You are prepared. The other half will come when you least expect it. It's as if you stand up on a dark night and shout into the distance, "I am ready!" You don't know when that message will be heard by someone now unknown to you, who will answer, "So am I!"

EXERCISE

Summarize your learnings from this chapter. How do you want to act on them? What further questions do you have for yourself?

On your Summary Page for this chapter, write the characteristics of the workplace that call forth the best in you.

The process of personal or organizational change is marked by working hard and letting go. You have worked hard to raise your consciousness and perhaps to institute change. Now let go, and allow events to take their course for a while. Practice letting go by engaging in one of your favorite relaxing activities. Enjoy!

Create Your BEST WORK

If you keep doing little things about it, your dream, which was amorphous at first, will begin to take shape, like a statue emerging from a chunk of marble. — Carolyn Jabs

1 Take a Look at Where You've Come

Two people hike along a mountain trail. They agree to take a break and appreciate the view. Perched on a granite outcropping, they survey the scene—the village below, and then the forest, the surrounding peaks, the sky, and the ribbon of water winding its way through the valley. "What a panorama!" says one. "Yeah, and look how far we've come!" exclaims the other.

After a few moments, one says, "Let's check our bearings." Pulling out a map, they look at where they've come and then chart the next leg of their journey. Finally, getting up and stretching, one says, "OK, time to get moving."

You're on a journey of vocational exploration and enrichment. Now, as you come to the end of your guided tour, it is time to review what you've done, allow that totality to inform work choices, and then consider how to keep momentum going to express more of what you value in work. This is what is involved in our next step:

Create your BEST WORK.

Focused on both the present and the future, this chapter invites you to apply discoveries you've made to vocational searches you pursue or the work you now do. Segment 1 helps you look at how far you've come. Segment 2 offers a process to keep you focused on achieving your best. Segment 3 looks at how to develop strategies that deal with blocks toward creating our best work. Segment 4 considers the importance of balancing work with the rest of life. Segment 5 reminds us to celebrate progress in our quest for meaningful work. And Segment 7 cheers us on as we foster work from the heart in ourselves, our organizations, and society.

By using some of this book's processes, Diana, a lively woman in her mid-thirties, gained fresh insights. An accountant with excellent computer skills, she's the one at Safeway who makes sure that everyone in her region is paid on time and that proper deductions are taken for each employee. "It's a great job—I know that," she exclaimed. "But I'm tired of spending so much time in front of the computer. I'd like to work more with people."

To gain an overview of her discoveries, she summarized them in the following chart:

My Clarities and Commitments

The *gifts* I want to use:
- Commitment to people's growth
- Group facilitation skills
- Knowledge of financial workings of my organization

The *meaning* I want to incorporate:
- People who are growing personally and vocationally bring satisfaction to themselves and to their work.

The *parameters* that shape my choices:
- Make over $40,000
- Full-time
- Stay in Safeway system if possible

The *vocational dream* I am exploring:
- Human resource training in Safeway or another organization

The *people* who support my efforts . . .

"When I lined up my learnings like this, I saw that I could start right now where I am to use my group facilitation skills to help people grow. I'm asked to train new people, to manage work load, and to solve client problems. These are times to help people grow. I hadn't seen that before. I was so totally focused on getting the payroll completed."

Diana's summary helped her concentrate on the future as well.

"I'd like to explore a career switch to human resource training. There are people in that department at Safeway who can help me start down that path. Meanwhile, I'm committed to using now the gifts I've identified. Also I figured out the salary I'd like to work toward. Just focusing on these insights energizes me toward the future."

Diana was delighted to find in the words of Rumi, a thirteenth-century poet, a wonderful description of what was beginning to happen more fully for her: "Let the beauty of what you love be what you do."

> **EXERCISE**
>
> To sense progress made, gather the work you've done with each chapter —your statements, action plans, and Summary Pages. If necessary, update the Summary Pages.
>
> Then arrange them on a tabletop or on the floor. Let the total picture of what you've learned affect you. Notice the clarity you've gained and the commitments you intend to make to help you do your best work now or in the future.
>
> Create, as Diana did, a summary chart. Title it "My Clarities and Commitments." Reflect on what this summary means to you related to present and future work. Describe this in a separate statement.

2 Focus on the Future with the Present Well in Mind

Robert Fritz, author of *The Path of Least Resistance*, has spent many years studying the attitudes and activities of exceptionally creative people.[1] His discoveries can help us create the kind of work we really want to do.

He learned that we adopt one of two stances toward life. Either we respond and react to circumstances (the reactive mode), or we create the results we want (the creative mode). People whose work is truly productive and satisfying approach life with creativity. They imagine the results they want to achieve, then allow circumstances to shape their path toward those results.

Successful athletes do this. World-class cyclist Greg LeMond, for example, goes over his long-distance routes in meticulous detail. He knows them like the palm of his hand. In his mind's eye he visualizes himself rounding every curve and mounting each hill with peak precision and grace, ending with a blast across the finish line in record time.

How do creative people know the result they want to achieve? Fritz gives the obvious but surprising answer: they make it up! Greg LeMond makes up a picture of himself finishing first. Writer Alice Walker, through her imagination, makes up the characters that people her novels.

We may not be Greg LeMond or Alice Walker, but all of us have the ability to make things up. When we use our imaginations to envision the work we want to do, we find the energy and guidance for it to happen.

Fritz points out that there is a natural conflict between vision (what you want) and reality (what you have). That conflict can cause anxiety that pulls us down and away from our vision or it can cause creative tension that moves us forward toward realizing our vision.

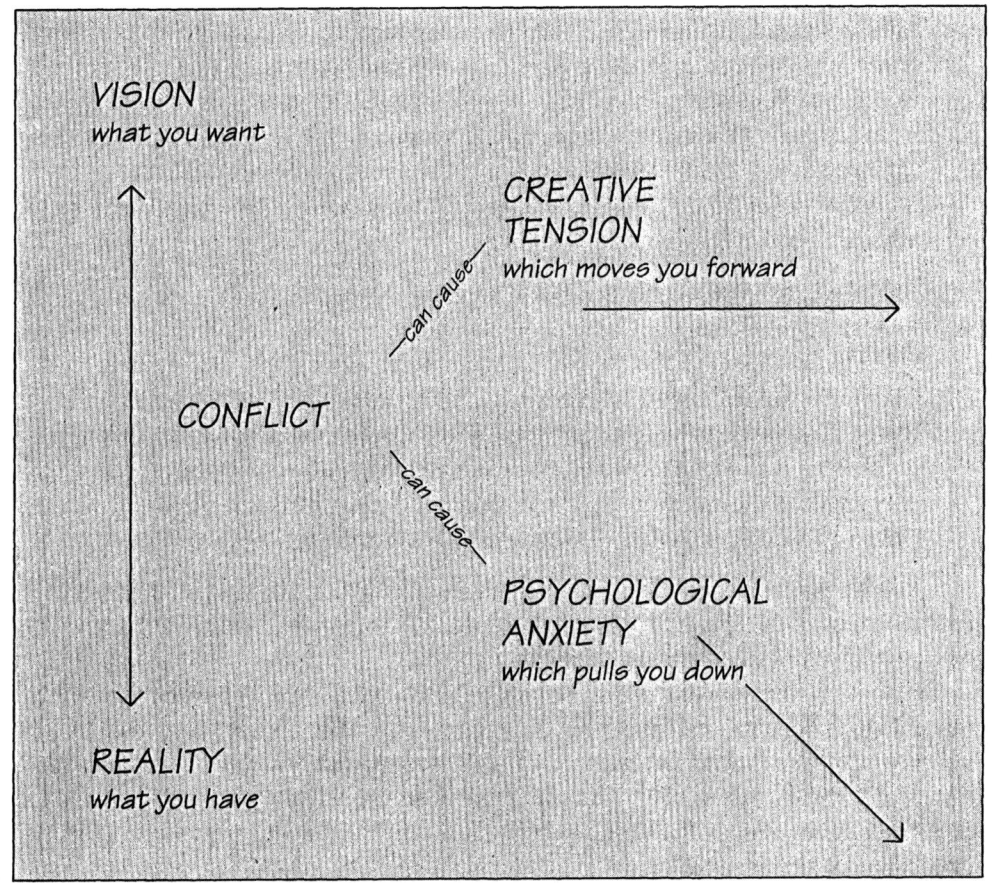

We can choose whether the conflict between vision and reality will move us forward or pull us down. Our choice to move forward depends, according to Fritz, on making two fundamental choices: to be healthy and free, and to be the primary, creative force in our own lives.

Fritz offers a process to move forward and achieve the results we desire. In brief, it includes picturing your vision, describing your current reality, re-choosing the vision, allowing steps to surface that could change your reality, and then taking at least one step toward what you want. Included in the activity section are more detailed instructions for you to use this process.

Here's how Diana worked with three of Fritz's steps in her own life. First, she wrote down her vision as if it were actually happening.

My Vision for Future Work

I am a skilled trainer at Safeway responsible for offering courses about company benefits, productivity increase, and team building. This work makes me feel great. My gifts and creativity are used every day. I love interacting with people and seeing folks increase their skills. Requests for my services come in all the time—I'm busy, people need me. Consistent feedback tells me that employees work better and feel better after taking my courses.

She then described in writing the situation she was in.

Reality

Currently my job requires monthly accounting and computer skills—things I know but don't want to do anymore. I've taken one course in training and loved it, but I have no other formal preparation for a career in human resource development. The training division at Safeway is currently full. It does not need another person.

Diana attempted to see her vision and reality as two sides of a greater truth. She decided to let the two dialogue within herself for a while so that next steps would surface in their own time.

The next day while driving to work, Diana pondered what she had written about vision and current reality. A communication course she had taken last year popped into her mind. "When I was practicing those communication skills, I felt super," she mused. "Everyone told me how well I did—and also how great I looked while I was in the course. One person even said he had never seen me so happy."

The weekend came along. While tidying up the house, another thought occurred: "When I'm learning something new, I feel so alive. I'd like to take more courses." She then began thinking about course fees. Would Safeway be willing to pay her tuition? She planned to ask, but even if the answer was no,

Diana knew she wanted to go ahead, even if she had to pay the bill herself. She began thinking ahead. "As much as I'd like to stay at Safeway if I possibly could, I should begin to learn about other job possibilities in training." She was amazed at how many ideas for next steps surfaced almost automatically, while she was doing something else. Excitedly, she wrote down the next logical step to move her toward a career in training:

Action

I will obtain listings of human resource development courses in my area to see what is available. Then I'll sign up for the one that most catches my fancy and is in a workable timeframe.

The beauty of Fritz's process is that it focuses on a positive vision for the future. Too often, obstacles wield more influence than they should. When you envision a future outcome that excites you, energy rises. Steps occur that will move you toward that future.

Fritz's process helps you envision choices as life evolves. In one of our seminars, Sandy took a ball and, rolling it forward, said, "This is the way my life is—it unfolds as it goes. I'm not a goal maker, but I do want to grow in my work." Fritz's process honors that feeling of evolution and combines it with imagining desired results in a way that helps not only to track progress but to create it.

It takes advantage of the technique of "futuring," which organizations use for planning. Consultant Marvin Weisbord found that when a company engages in long-range planning, step-by-step, it tends to get bogged down. "We are here and want to move to there. What steps can we take to accomplish that?" This approach wears everyone out, he finds. Weisbord also discovered that the vision of a charismatic CEO, no matter how astute, is not owned by others in the company when it is simply "passed down from above." What really ignites people at all levels is futuring. Get "all the people into the room"—janitors, bureau chiefs, clerks, and top executives, Weisbord counsels. Then imagine together "where we want to be ten years from now." Finally, flesh out the steps that would move everyone toward that future.[2]

What is useful for organizations benefits individuals as well. When we "get everyone into the room"—our sensible, imaginative, cautious, and wild and crazy selves—we bring our whole capacity to creating the work we really want to do. By tracking results as they occur, we produce insight that keeps us moving toward our dream, whether it be a new project or a different kind of work altogether.

To create momentum toward the results you want, use the following steps:

1. Know what you want.
2. Know what you have.
3. Take action to create what you want.
4. Track results effectively.
5. Use unwanted results to define more effective next steps.

EXERCISE

Give special attention to describing your vision. Polish it until it you really like it. Take a few minutes to write a brief version of this vision. Entitle it "My Vision for Future Work." This is labor you really want to do, your particular work from the heart. It may be a better way of doing your present job or new work altogether. Place this brief vision on a blank piece of paper. Decorate it if you wish. Bring it to the Gathering.

Then proceed with this outline of Fritz's process. Move through its steps at least once. As Diana did, give yourself several days to do this. Alternate "focused time" when you take pencil in hand to write your thoughts with "down time" when thoughts can jell or surface involuntarily.

VISION/REALITY PROCESS

To prepare for participating in this process, make these fundamental choices:

1. I choose to be healthy and free.
2. I am the primary, creative force in my life.

Next, write a brief, clear statement in response to each bulleted item below.

Picture Your Vision:

What do you really want?

- Describe this fully so you'll recognize it when it happens.
- State it in an upbeat manner *as if it is happening*. Write the complete result you desire.

Describe Current Reality:

What is going on?

- State current reality (what you have) related to vision.

Choose to Create:

What do I want? (You are asking this again.)

- Restate, re-choose vision.

What do I want to create? (This seems redundant. But allow the slightly different wording to kick up a stronger statement.)

- State in fresh language.

Brainstorm Possible Steps:

What actions could I take to create the results I want?

- Allow all the actions you can think of to surface; jot them down.

Decide on One or More Steps to Take Now:

What next steps will I take first?

- Choose what is do-able now that will change situation.

Take Action:

- Take one or more of the do-able steps.

Track results.

What happened?

- List steps taken.
- List results received.

The results received will change your perception of your vision, current reality, and/or next steps. You then are in a different position. Building on new information gathered, repeat the process as necessary to guide you toward the results you wish to create.

3 Confusion— Prelude to Creation

Fritz's process brings clarity and momentum to creating great work. But sometimes, we are too stuck to throw ourselves into it. We might have created visions before that were not realized. This hurts our ability to conceive or believe in a fresh vision. Or, even if we can articulate a vision, the circumstances of reality might be so overwhelming that we feel blocked. Jaime expressed this predicament at one of our workshops.

"I know the kind of work I'd like, but I'm scared to do what it takes to get there." said Jaime. "I'm a high school English teacher. To do that well takes everything I have. It's so exhausting. But I'd really love to give up teaching and earn a living with my art."

"Well, why don't you?" asked another seminar participant.

"It's taken me so long to get to where I am. I'm thirty-five, have a nice apartment, a car. For the first time, I have a decent income and don't have to live on the margin. It's not easy to throw that away. On the other hand, I know if I keep this job, it will kill me. I am, frankly, afraid to change. Where will I find the courage?"

Jaime knew what he wanted to do but was immobilized by fear, uncertainty, and doubt. The seminar participants came up with some interesting responses.

A retired person in his seventies said, "I find risk taking to be an acquired skill. It takes practice. First, I take little risks, then large ones. Slowly, my ability to risk is strengthened."

"Right now, my predominant feeling is uncertainty," responded a young editor who wanted to explore the possibility of establishing her own marketing business. "At this point, I'm taking classes at the community college to see if it's a fit. I'm letting myself flow with the uncertainty. That seems OK. I don't have to know the specifics yet."

"For me," said a lawyer, who was in the process of becoming a professional photographer/author, "it's been more like gradually easing into the shallow end of the pool as I'm ready. Slowly, my hobby of traveling and photography, along with my appreciation of nature and sacred sites, has gathered more and more strength. First my photographs began appearing in other people's books. Then a publisher advanced me money to produce my own text and photographs. Now I have the confidence that if I set off for a swim, the water will buoy me up."

Each of these people made different points about how to meet the unknown and move through the chaos of confusion to creation. The following is a review of their points with some additional ones included. They are offered as encouragement as you contemplate your next move.

Take a small risk at a time. Sometimes the step you contemplate is just too big to start you off. Break it into several do-able pieces.

Stay with the uncertainty. Wait it out. This is a natural state of affairs and nothing to be too alarmed about. It will pass. It's a little like being in a sandstorm: sometimes the best thing to do is fall down on the ground, wrap your robe about you, and wait until it's over. Eventually the force of the storm will subside.

Be open to help from others. The forces of fear or uncertainty may be strong enough to push you outside yourself to seek another's advice or encouragement. That is positive. That person may help you sort through confusion.

Take apart the blockage. A feeling of fear or confusion is like a conglomerate rock. Negative possibilities tend to stick to one another, as do the smaller stones in a larger conglomerate. The huge stone can weigh you down. Take out a rock hammer. Split the rock into its smaller pieces. Name them. Decide one at a time how you will address each component.

Gradually build up the thing you love. Perhaps Jaime's art skills are not strong enough to propel him into a new profession. That might be why he is hesitant to make the switch. Like the lawyer, he needs to move gradually, strengthening the skills he really wants to use before diving into a career change.

Turn the blockage into a question. Convert "I'm afraid" (blockage) into "How can I gain more courage to do what I want?" (question). Then live with the question, allowing the answers to unfold in their own time.

Develop the perspective of humor. Ram Dass, when asked about his attitude toward inner fears, replied, "In all the years of taking drugs, being a Freudian, being a therapist, meditating, having a guru, Sufi dancing, whatever, I haven't gotten rid of one neurosis yet. The only difference is that instead of these monsters, there are these little schmoes now, and I just invite them in for tea."[3]

The process of creating a new way to work or a new kind of work to do will feel blocked at times. That is to be expected. The important thing is to find ways around these obstacles.

> **EXERCISE**
>
> As you contemplate creating the work you want to do in Segment 2, do any attitudes or feelings arise that cause you to feel immobilized? If so, name them. For example, "I feel blocked by . . ." "I'm afraid of . . ."
>
> Review the strategies described above for addressing these blocks. Plan to carry out two that seem most appropriate at this time.
>
> Describe in writing the strategies you want to use and how you will carry them out. For example, Diana wrote:
>
> *Blockage*
>
> I'm afraid of public speaking. It scares me to death. Yet the training job I want involves speaking in front of other people.
>
> *Strategies to Address My Fear*
>
> 1. Convert this blockage into a question: How can I develop courage to speak in front of people?
> 2. Be open to help from others: I'm going to start asking people how they developed skill in public speaking.

Balance Work with the Rest of Life

"I find that I enjoy every aspect of life—including work, if I have the time to engage in it with care," said Tom, a mechanical engineer and father of three. "The trick is to find the time for each piece that is important to me."

That is most people's challenge. An interesting approach to time management was introduced to Tom by his friends, Alice, a freelance writer, and Tad, a retired oil corporation executive. "Write down your lifetime goals,"

Alice suggested. "Now write some possible activities you could do to achieve each goal." When he had completed that, Tad continued, "Finally, think about the next month. Choose activities related to each goal that you could do during this month."

Tom readily thought of four lifetime goals:

- To find work that is international in scope and contributes to other countries, but allows me to live here in the States.
- To enjoy my family and learn from them.
- To keep fit and have some adventures.
- To develop a vital spiritual life.

Some activities for each goal began to occur to him. To prepare for international work, he could brush up on his Spanish. He also could subscribe to an international work opportunity newsletter. As a family activity, he wanted to go to the library with his kids to select books that he and they would enjoy reading together. For adventure, he put a box in his bureau drawer for adventure ideas that appealed to him as he heard about them from friends or from reading. The articulation of his spiritual goal motivated him to start attending a downtown church that was known for its work in neighborhood revitalization.

"What surprised me about this simple time management scheme," he told his friends, "is that it does not take a lot of effort to think up or even carry out activities related to my goals. Once I had the goals in place, ways to implement them occurred rather spontaneously. When the kids wanted me to take them canoeing, I knew that could easily become an adventure if I brought that spirit to it."

Alice agreed. "I've found it a wonderful way to stay focused on what I really care about and to achieve a good interplay between my various activities."

"What I've realized is that simply reading over my list from time to time reminds me to take advantage of opportunities when they occur to move toward my goals," added Tad. "And I find that my goals change a bit as I change. It's fun to see them evolve."

Note how similar Alice and Tad's suggestions are to Robert Fritz's visioning process, which was applied to vocational dreams in the last segment. Both can be used with various parts of your life. By doing so, you value each part and make room for each to enrich the others.

> **EXERCISES**
>
> Which part of your nonwork life is asking for attention now? Listen to its wishes. Then respond by creating two next steps that will create balance in your life.

5 Celebrate Success and New Commitments

At their fortieth high school reunion, former classmates mingle, recall old connections, and give an account of their current situations. Grandchildren and retirement plans are big topics. Don, the local middle school principal and city councilman, is asked how he likes his jobs. "I love them," he replies. "There's always a new challenge. I'm very happy to be in this sort of work." Don had an upbeat attitude in high school and has maintained it all his life.

Don's lifetime of enthusiastic dedication makes one ask how he does it. Or more personally, How can we keep our fire burning brightly?

Two people who know a lot about this are John Graham and Anne Medlock. Founders of the Giraffe Project, whose aim is to inspire people "to stick their necks out for the common good," they recognize and celebrate folks like Earl Zela Aldridge.[4] Shocked by the explosion of a Jersey City chemical plant, Aldridge got himself appointed environmental inspector. He put in "eighteen-hour days, staking out dump sites, collecting volumes of data and identifying ninety illegal dumps." Despite the opposition of the organizations who continue to dump, Aldridge continues his crusade to leave for the children of his town "the cleanest city of the world."[5]

John Graham and Anne Medlock operate the Giraffe Project on a shoestring, and often in the red. What keeps their spirits up?

"Celebrating every success," writes John. "Particularly those that may seem too small or insignificant to even recognize as 'successes'—like the letterhead coming back from the printer on time or the official you've been trying to get on the phone actually calling you back."[6]

Most of us are not used to congratulating ourselves as often as John and Anne recommend. Perhaps we're obsessed with scaling the peak and don't stop to affirm how well we packed our rucksack. By recognizing steps taken and results achieved, however minuscule, we gain momentum for taking the next step, and the next. "Each success seems to make the next one easier, and big successes seem to follow an appreciation of smaller ones," writes Graham. "Resources appear out of nowhere. Obstacles fall as if by magic. Celebration is a way to keep the dice hot, to keep the magic going. To switch metaphors, imagine that celebrating success is pump-priming—say thanks for every trickle and a real stream can follow."[7]

Yes, there may be mistakes, failures, fruitful opportunities missed along the way. None of us is omniscient—the way unfolds before us, and we can't avoid those times of going off course. The challenge is to recognize when we're deflected away from our particular vision of meaningful work and then to make a quick adjustment and recovery.

Robert Fritz suggests that each recognition of failure can be the most important moment of our lives, because it is then that we adjust the vision to correspond more closely with reality. John Graham echoes the thought: "If things take a turn you don't expect or plan for, accept the shifts as part of the creative process that was simply beyond your capacity to know at the time. Welcome it. Adjust the vision. Enjoy your flexibility and the results it can help you achieve."[8]

Take time to celebrate your clarities and commitments, the steps you intend to take toward your future work life, and the hopes you have for new ventures.

EXERCISE

Look over your work from Segments 1, 2, 3, and 4. Describe where you hope to be in six months and in one year. Include specifics that will help you get there. Here is what Diana wrote:

Hopes and Intentions

By next June I would like to have enough information to decide whether I should stay with Safeway or put major effort into exploring other companies. I will also have taken one more training course. By next January I'd like to decide whether a move from accounting to a career in training is realistic for me.

6 Gathering

Purpose: To affirm what has been accomplished and to complete the time together

Leaders bring: Candles and matches

Everyone bring:

>   My Clarities and Commitments from Segment 1
>   My Vision for Future Work from Segment 2
>   Strategies to overcome blockages from Segment 3
>   Next steps from Segment 4
>   Hopes and Intentions from Segment 5

WARM-UP (EVERYONE)
30 MINUTES

1. Place vision statements in the center of your circle around a lighted candle.
2. Take them in—and ask each other about them.
3. Read your vision statements to each other, holding a lighted candle as you do so.
4. Celebrate being part of a circle of vision.

RECOGNITION AND AFFIRMATION (EVERYONE)
40 MINUTES

1. Each person take a few minutes to review the work you brought to the Gathering. Prepare to share the parts of your final work that carry the most energy now. When everyone is ready, give each person time to describe

- clarities and commitments (not all of them, just those you feel most energized by)
- strategies to overcome blockages
- next steps to bring balance into your life
- hopes for where you want to be six months and a year from now

2. Exchange feedback.

APPRECIATION AND CLOSING (EVERYONE)
20 MINUTES

1. Each person share how the group sessions have been for you. Include what you have appreciated and what you wish had been different (i.e., ideas for improvement next time).

2. Close with encouraging words to one another as you move out on your own.

3. Read the following for a send-off:

   Be a Giraffe.
   Stick your neck out for the common good.
   Choose,
   and continually choose
   work that uses the best of you
   to make the world a better place.
   When you go off course,
   adjust quickly.
   And celebrate, celebrate, CELEBRATE
   every success along the way!

7 Keep Flying!

You've celebrated your work together with your group or your partner. Now the challenge is to keep the celebratory mood going as you move on without the communal structure of the Gathering sessions to spur you on. Here are some ideas:

- Place your vision for future work on the Summary Page.
- Take a well-earned rest for a while.

- Put some dates on the calendar to mark when you'll take next steps.
- Plan a dinner out with your partner or group members to catch up after a month.

Do one thing to give yourself the huge pat on the back you deserve for good work well done.

Appendix A

How to Make Money and Do What You Love

Is it really possible to make money and do what you love? Yes, it is. But it isn't always easy to figure out how. Here are five different ways people have solved the problem of combining money and meaningful work.

Immediate Change. Upon leaving the Air Force in his mid-forties, Bob wanted to use his military experience in the cause of peace. He created a résumé that clearly put forward his intention. Networking many times a week produced leads that eventually materialized into a job as legislative aide for a United States senator. Bob knew he wanted a change and went after it with focus and intensity, landing a job with salary comparable to what he had been earning.

Gradual Change. Chuck, an administrative law judge, was ready to leave his job but needed its salary to put his kids through college. His future focus was clear: he wanted to become a counselor, specializing in men's issues. However, he had no training in this field. Now enrolled in a night graduate program in social work, he's immersed in study he loves and is continuing full time in his present job. The pressure for it to be more than it is has receded. Since moving toward a different future, he actually finds he likes his present job more!

Transition Work. An excellent computer programmer, Kevin realized he wanted more people-centered work. He settled on the goal of becoming a human development trainer in personal growth. But he's taking it a step at a time. He has left his computer job and has started in a new position training people in computer programming. This places him in the field of training, but not yet teaching the subjects he loves. That might be his next step, perhaps with some graduate study in between.

Settle for Less. Jo has the kind of work Kevin wants, but feels a new call to be a pastor. She has taken several steps. First, she began saving all she could for seminary training. Second, with the help of a financial adviser, she trimmed down her financial needs and decided what she could do without. Then she sold her home and furniture and moved into a rented room. "I actually like traveling light much more than I thought I would," she reports. She's on her way toward her new vocation, having entered seminary this fall.

Stay and Enrich What You Have. As an accountant, Lynn helps middle-income people keep their finances straight. She likes this work and is earning the salary she needs. She also has a dream of working directly with disadvantaged children. Recently she convinced her company to allow her to develop a school mentoring program. Accountants in her firm now give an average of three hours weekly in math tutoring to inner-city children. This has brought much satisfaction to everyone who is involved. It has helped Lynn realize her dream without leaving the job she wants to keep.

Appendix B

Interviewing for Information
What It Is and How to Go About It

The technique called interviewing for information comes from the employment counseling field. If you are looking for work in a particular field, you do not get far by simply sending résumés to personnel offices or responding to classified advertisements in newspapers. Like the best houses for sale that are snatched up before being listed, the best jobs are often learned about through inside contacts.

Interviewing for information is a well-known technique for fact-gathering related to a job search. It can also be used to search for ways to enrich the workplace or explore other areas of life. In a broad sense, interviewing for information can be defined as a formal technique for gathering information necessary for decision making.

When you do interviewing of this sort, it is important to be as clear as possible about what you hope to receive from the person with whom you are meeting. Depending on whether you are researching a new field or enriching the work you have, you should think through the kinds of *concrete information* you want. For example:

- People or organizations to contact.
- Books to read.
- Leads on jobs.
- Enrichment ideas.
- Training information.
- Conferences or workshops to attend.

- Related fields or organizations to be aware of.
- Other clues.

Be sure you obtain and jot down as much concrete information as possible.

Be aware that your *feelings* may be "all over the place" before, during, and after the interviews. Your feelings are important indicators, so try to read the messages in them. If you don't like the person you are interviewing, why? If you feel let down, why? If you are excited, why? A natural feeling that may occur is a sense of being "less than" the person you interview because that person is in a more secure position than you are. Recognize that this happens, talk it over with a friend, but don't give more weight to it than it deserves.

Interviewing for information is useful if done well. That is why it is good to have a thorough knowledge of all the steps involved, as well as practice in using them. Then you can adapt the technique for informal use. Here are the steps:

Preparation

1. Choose the person/organization to interview. Start with someone who will be easy to approach—for example, a person you already know or someone a friend knows. Practice with those people. Slowly move to people who present more of a challenge, such as someone you don't know or a person who is more experienced than you are.

2. Obtain information beforehand about the person/organization. Seek this yourself or ask the person you will be meeting to send it to you in advance of the interview.

3. Establish the date, time, and length of the interview. Asking for an hour may be appropriate, but a great deal can be learned in only ten minutes if you're focused. The person might not have time for an interview but might be able to assist you right then on the phone. So be prepared for this.

4. Prepare in writing a brief statement about yourself and the purpose of the interview:
- Who you are
- Where you are in your search

Interviewing for Information

- Why you have chosen this person
- What kind of information or help you need

This will help you avoid two common pitfalls: speaking too long about yourself or assuming the person knows about you and your purpose without being clearly told.

5. Prepare your questions in writing. Divide them into two parts:

Ask about the individual. For example:

(For the Searcher)
- How did you get into this work?
- What training and experience did you have?
- What are your duties and responsibilities?
- What do you like (and not like) about your work?

(For the Job Enricher)
- How did you initiate change at work?
- How did you deal with the resistance?

Ask for the person's help for your situation. For example:

(For the Searcher)
- With my background in _____ and _____, what additional training or experience do I need to move into this field?
- What kinds of job possibilities are there in this field for someone with my skills?

(For the Job Enricher)
- If you were in my situation, how would you deal with _____?

Execution

1. Check the amount of time you have for the interview. Verify that what you agreed to on the phone is the amount of time still available. If it isn't, ask the person how much time he or she can allow for your conversation now.

2. Go over in summary form what you want to cover and why. Tell briefly who you are, where you are in your life, why you have chosen to talk with this person, what you hope to find out, and why you want to find it out. You may want to share your entire line of questioning with the person, so he or she will know how much you want to cover in the allotted time. For example, "I have several questions to ask about your experience. That should take about ten minutes. Then I'd like to use another fifteen minutes to ask some questions about my own direction." Consider showing the person your résumé, if you have one, in order to give a quick picture of your situation.

3. If you want to tape the interview, this would be the time to ask. Be sure to give the person the freedom to say no.

4. Remember to take good notes. Some people write their questions beforehand, leaving space to write the answers as they are given.

5. Remember that you asked for the interview and you are in control of the time. It is easy for the person being interviewed to linger on points that may not interest you. You must keep the person on track in appropriate ways. For example, "That is helpful, but I would like more information about . . ."

6. Keep track of the time. Five minutes before you are to end, start bringing the interview to a close. This is the time to ask the person if you can use his or her name in making other contacts. Do this only if it seems appropriate.

7. Thank the person and leave promptly. If you feel you may want to see the person again or call later for additional clarification, ask if that would be possible.

8. Go over your notes. As soon as possible (perhaps before you go on to your next activity!), look at your notes and fill in points that you did not write down.

Evaluation: What Did It Mean?

1. What specific leads did you receive?
- People, organizations to *talk* with.
- Publications to *read*.

- Opportunities to *experience* the vocational dream you are exploring.
- *Enrichment* ideas for present work.

2. Which were pertinent, helpful, or motivating to you? Which do you need to discard?

3. What did you learn about the interviewing process?

The execution of the interview: Did your questions elicit the information you needed? Is there anything you can improve?

Your feelings while in the interview: What feelings were generated that might have a message for you? What is the message?

4. What clues for your future direction did you receive from this interview?

Follow-up

1. Write a letter to thank the person. Include any information you promised to send, anything you wish the person to remember about you or what happened, and any word about follow-up you intend to do. Naturally, you may not have immediate plans to follow through on all the ideas you received. You may want to point out steps you're taking that build on the interview.

2. Look over the notes of your interview and decide which leads you want to pursue or which ideas you want to build on. Think through the big picture. Where do you go from here? What next moves are suggested by your experience with the person and your own energy level?

Write-up

1. Whether realization of vocational dreams is to be accomplished through enrichment or job change, it is useful to *write a summary of the interview.* This should include the name, address, phone number, and position of the person; the date of the interview; why you interviewed the person; a summary of the concrete information you obtained; and any feelings or questions you want to remember.
2. Consider writing important data on a card for ready access.

Interviewing for information is a challenge to do well. Once you have learned how to do it in a formal way, you will find that you can use it informally in many situations. It is an art. You will always be learning how to do it more effectively.

Appendix C

Training Decisions

Some Factors to Consider

There are many valid reasons to get further training. Here are some of them:

1. Academic knowledge. You may want to gain academic grounding in a specific field of study, such as urban planning, art therapy, or public relations. This could be done through taking one or two courses or perhaps a full-degree program.

2. Skills. Specific how-to skills, such as drafting, group process, accounting, or low-income housing advocacy, can be part of degree programs, but they are often taught in separate workshops or short programs.

3. Credentialing. Certain fields require specific types of training to enter at particular levels; what kind and how much varies a great deal. It is important to find out what is required in your own field of interest and not assume that just because you have management training, for example, you will be credentialed to work in all management positions.

4. Affiliation. You may want to be affiliated with a recognized center in the field of your interest. For example, conflict management is now taught at several universities; to complete one of these programs trains you in a recognized approach related to that field.

5. Contacts. It is important to meet people who are active in fields that interest you. A way to do this is to participate in training in which they are also involved either as leaders or as participants.

6. Status and recognition. A way to be accepted as competent and available in a field is to attend training offered by people with known reputations in that field. They see your ability in action and can perhaps help you find the work you want to do.

7. Discernment. To decide whether a particular field is worth pursuing, take some short-term training in that field. You'll get a firsthand feel for it and the people involved before making a deeper commitment.

8. Change and newness. To bring this into your work, take some training in your own field or a related or even not-so-related field. New content and approaches bring refreshment to what you do.

Practical Issues to Take into Account

In deciding which is the best training for you, there are several issues to consider. Some are related to the reasons for training just mentioned. Which programs will offer you the knowledge, skills, credentialing, affiliation, contacts, status, discernment, or newness that you desire now? Here are other issues to consider:

1. Money. How much does the program cost? How much can I afford to invest in my own training considering the return on my investment? What financial aid is available?

2. Timing. Do the length of the program and the time of day and time in the year it's held fit my situation?

3. Location. Is the location convenient or attractive to me?

4. Leadership. Do the program's leaders have a good reputation? Can they offer me what I want in a way that is motivating?

Steps Toward Making a Wise Decision

The more care you take with your decision making, the better served you will be by your choice. Consider taking the following steps:

1. Assess your needs. Review the "Factors to Consider" section and recognize clearly what you need from training and why. Do as much research as possible on training alternatives available to you.

2. Talk with participants in programs you are considering. Be specific. Ask to see the books they read; discuss the labs and activities of the program; find out their perspectives on the pros and cons of the program.

3. Be aware of what training is valued by those with whom you would like to work. Ask for advice and suggestions from those who are supporting you in the field, that is, mentors, advisers, people with whom you have conducted informational interviews.

4. Interview the people who run the programs. Remember, they usually want your business and may be prepared to be flexible, but it is up to you to be imaginative. Without a nudge, the people in charge will usually go by the rules and approach things from the perspective of their program, not your unique vocation or experience. Here are some questions you might ask:

> What is the purpose of the program?
>
> How long does it take?
>
> How much classroom time is involved; how much homework?
>
> How much does it cost?
>
> What credentials will I earn if I participate?
>
> What help is available for helping graduates find jobs?
>
> What are the components of the program?
> > lectures
> > lab
> > papers
> > practicum
> > student-teacher interaction
>
> Is it possible to obtain names of some recent participants?

After each interview, summarize it in writing. You will want to include:

> Name of program
>
> Date of interview
>
> Name and position of the person you interviewed
>
> Phone number
>
> Address
>
> Summary of what you learned about cost, location, features, etc.

If you interview a participant in the program, incorporate that person's observations in your summary.

5. Compare programs you are considering. Talk options over with a friendly adviser.

Additional Points to Consider

1. Training is a lifelong process. There is no ultimate or perfect training experience at a particular time. Each has advantages and drawbacks.

2. Some people seek universally understood qualifying training experiences. Others (because of the nature of their field) recognize that there are no universally accepted training experiences. Training in some fields is more tightly regulated than in others.

3. Some training decisions cannot and should not be rushed. To test the waters, it may be better to undergo less demanding training, such as workshops and short-term events, before entering a demanding degree program.

4. Sometimes a person wants to skip some steps in training. People who do not have a full undergraduate degree may want to go right into a graduate-level program. It takes a good deal of preparation to make a strong case for such a move. Here are some suggestions:

Find out what the formal requirements are beforehand; do some investigating about the policy on flexibility.

Talk about your situation with people who know that system; find out what they are looking for in a candidate, such as experience in the field, background reading and study, ability to handle the work load.

Document your case and present it well, with emphasis on what program coordinators are looking for—address all those issues. For example, if an academic graduate department wants to know whether you can handle the course content intellectually, be prepared to say you have read and understood one or more of the texts used.

Be prepared to negotiate. You might want to skip undergraduate work altogether, whereas the program might require a few undergraduate courses in certain fields. You might propose that you take a lighter load, or ask that they accept you on probation.

5. It is important to trust yourself and your own sense of timing in making good training decisions.

6. Don't hesitate to ask for help with these decisions. They are difficult and require a lot of information to make well.

7. To keep abreast of training opportunities, get on the mailing lists of various training groups. Keep a file of their offerings and consider how they meet your requirements for training.

8. Keep in mind that there are many different types of training, all of which have validity in the right situation:

    Self-study
    Continuing education programs
    Special skills training
    Degree programs
    Apprenticeship or internship

Appendix D

ACTION ITEM[1]

The Cure for Burnout: Refueling Your Tank

What percentage of the time do you get an adequate amount of each of these?

	Area	0	10	20	30	40	50	60	70	80	90	100%
1.	Proper rest											
2.	Good nutrition											
3.	Daily "non-stressed" exercise											
4.	Time alone											
5.	Time to read and learn											
6.	Spiritual growth											
7.	Intimacy and love											
8.	Fun, joy, and play											
9.	Quality time with family and friends											
10.	New interests or hobbies											
11.	Regular and frequent vacations											
12.	Sense of purpose											

Choose one area that is low and creatively brainstorm some ways to increase the time devoted to this area by 10% over the next month. The purpose in setting a modest goal is to be sure it is attainable. Set yourself up to win. Let both your intuition and your logic tell you which is most important to improve. Frequently, a small improvement in one critical area can make a big difference toward moving you back to whole-brained balance.

Notes

Epigraph: Studs Terkel, *Working: People Talk About What They Do All Day and How They Feel About What They Do* (New York: Pantheon Books, 1974), xxix.

CHAPTER 1. OFFER GIFTS YOU WANT TO USE

Epigraph: Joseph Campbell with Bill Moyers, *The Power of Myth* (New York: Doubleday, 1988), 151.

1. Lois Robbins, *Waking Up in the Age of Creativity* (Santa Fe, NM: Bear & Company, 1985), chaps. 4, 5.
2. Robbins, *Waking Up in the Age of Creativity*, 70.
3. Robbins, *Waking Up in the Age of Creativity*, 70.
4. Joan Smith, "Our Gifts: Joy and Responsibility," from a sermon given at Shrewsbury Community Church, Shrewsbury, Vermont.
5. Joseph Campbell, in *The Hero's Journey, Joseph Campbell*, edited by Phil Cousineau (San Francisco: HarperSanFrancisco, 1990), 19.
6. Campbell, in *The Hero's Journey*, 155.
7. Thomas Moore, *Care of the Soul* (New York: Harper Collins, 1992), 184.
8. Moore, *Care of the Soul*, 185.
9. Hyler Bracey, Jack Rosenblum, Aubrey Sanford, Roy Trueblood, *Managing from the Heart* (New York: Delacorte Press, 1990), 192.
10. Marsha Sinetar, "Right Livelihood in a Recession?" *Common Boundary*, July/August 1992, 41.
11. Sinetar, "Right Livelihood," 43.
12. Sinetar, "Right Livelihood," 43.

CHAPTER 2. INCORPORATE MEANING IN WORK

Epigraph: Brita L. Gill-Austern, "Awakening the Trusting Heart," *Keeping You Posted* 20, no. 7 (September 1985), 2 (published in New York by the Office of Communication, United Church of Christ).

1. Mario Cuomo, quoted by Judy Mann, "The Quest for Life's Meaning," *Washington Post Magazine*, 14 June 1985.
2. Gail Sheehy, *Pathfinders* (New York: Bantam Books, 1981), 15.
3. This summarizes some of the insights in Joanna Macy's book *Despair and Personal Power in the Nuclear Age* (Philadelphia: New Society Publishers, 1983).
4. Bruce Thomas, as recorded on "This Line Is Singin'" by the Freedom Song Network, 131 Mangels, San Francisco, CA 94131.
5. Matthew Fox, *Sheer Joy* (San Francisco: HarperSanFrancisco, 1992), 29.
6. Russell Schweickart, "No Frames, No Boundaries," in *Earth's Answer*, edited by William P. Marsh (New York: Lindisfarne Press, 1987), 11–12.
7. Studs Terkel, *Working: People Talk About What They Do All Day and How They Feel About What They Do* (New York: Pantheon Books, 1974), xxix.

8. Marilyn Ferguson, *The Aquarian Conspiracy* (Los Angeles: J. P. Tarcher, 1980), 109.
9. Carl G. Jung, *Memories, Dreams, Reflections* (New York: Vintage Books, 1965), 170.
10. Jung, *Memories, Dreams, Reflections*, 196.
11. Robert Bellah, Richard Madsen, William Sullivan, Ann Swidler, and Steven Tipton, *Habits of the Heart* (Berkeley: Univ. of California Press, 1985), 333.
12. Bellah et al, *Habits of the Heart*, 153, 154.
13. This exercise is adapted from one offered by Howard Hanger in "What Makes Your Life Worth Living," *Vision*, a newsletter published by Jubilee! Community, 46 Wall Street, Asheville, NC 28801.
14. Stan is one of our seminar participants. We have used excerpts from his writing in this section.
15. Jose Hobday, "The Medicine Bag," *Praying*, no. 28.
16. Peter Block, *The Empowered Manager* (San Francisco: Jossey-Bass, 1987), 99.
17. Block, *Empowered Manager*, 103.
18. Block, *Empowered Manager*, 189, 190.
19. Block, *Empowered Manager*, 189.

CHAPTER 3. DETERMINE HOW PARAMETERS SHAPE CHOICES

Epigraph: Norman Boucher and Laura Tennen, "In Search of Fulfillment," *New Age Journal*, May 1985, 27.

1. Ellen Goodman, *Close to Home* (New York: Simon & Schuster, 1979), 158–59.
2. Carolyn Jabs, "How to Kick a Dream into Action," *Self*, May 1986, 122.
3. Rom. 7:15. From the New Testament in Modern English, rev. ed., by J. B. Phillips (New York: Macmillan, 1958).
4. Elizabeth O'Connor, *Our Many Selves* (New York: Harper & Row, 1971).

CHAPTER 4. MOVE TOWARD VOCATIONAL DREAMS

Epigraph: Frank Barron, "Creativity: The Human Resource" (a pamphlet accompanying an exhibition researched and designed by The Burdick Group with the cooperation of the California Academy of Sciences through a grant from the Chevron Family of Companies, 1979), 152.

1. Another method for surfacing career options is John L. Holland's Self-Directed Search. This instrument enables you to assess your skills and to see the kinds of careers that use these skills. It can be ordered from Psychological Assessment Resources, Inc., Box 998, Odessa, FL 33556. To whet your appetite for this, see "The Party Exercise" in Richard Bolles's *What Color Is Your Parachute?*, 86–88.
2. Barbara Sher with Annie Gottlieb, *Wishcraft: How to Get What You Really Want* (New York: Viking Penguin, 1979), 152.
3. Peter M. Senge, *The Fifth Discipline* (New York: Doubleday/Currency, 1990).
4. Appendix B in Richard Bolles's *What Color Is Your Parachute?* contains an excellent list of such resources. Also, *The Whole Work Catalogue* contains a useful collection of resources. Order from The New Careers Center, 1515 23rd Street, Box 339-CT, Boulder, CO 80306.

5. Quoted by Charlotte Painter, *Gifts of Age: Portraits and Essays of 32 Remarkable Women* (San Francisco: Chronicle Books, 1985), 146.

CHAPTER 5. IDENTIFY PEOPLE TO HELP

Epigraph: Natasha Josefowitz, *Paths of Power* (Reading, MA: Addison-Wesley, 1980), 93.

1. Carla Hall, "For Father Hartke, A Fitting Farewell," *Washington Post Magazine*, 26 February 1986.
2. From a letter to the Reverend Phillips Brooks, dated June 8, 1891. Courtesy of the American Foundation for the Blind, New York, NY.
3. Alice Walker, *In Search of Our Mothers' Gardens* (New York: Harcourt Brace Jovanovich, 1983), xviii.
4. Joseph Campbell with Bill Moyers, *The Power of Myth* (New York: Doubleday, 1988), 120.
5. Margo Murray, *Beyond the Myths and Magic of Mentoring* (San Francisco: Jossey-Bass, 1991), 18.
6. Murray, *Beyond the Myths*, 18.
7. Most large cities have spiritual development centers that train spiritual guides or that can help you find a guide.
8. Colman McCarthy, *Inner Companions* (Washington, DC: Acropolis Books, 1975), 18.
9. Carol Van Sickle, "Jobless at 61: A Success Story," *Ms.*, October 1986, 66–67.
10. Van Sickle, "Jobless at 61," 66–67.
11. Van Sickle, "Jobless at 61," 68.

CHAPTER 6. FIND NOURISHMENT FOR YOUR WHOLE PERSON

Epigraph: Theodore Roszak, *Where The Wasteland Ends* (Winchester, MA: Faber & Faber, 1972), xxii.

1. Rollo May, *The Courage to Create* (New York: Bantam Books, 1976), 37.
2. Lois Robbins, *Waking Up in the Age of Creativity* (Santa Fe, NM: Bear & Company, 1985), 41.
3. Joseph Campbell with Bill Moyers, *The Power of Myth* (New York: Doubleday, 1988), 92.
4. James Fowler and Sam Keen, *Life Maps: Conversations on the Journey of Faith* (Dallas: Word, 1978), 120.
5. Marilyn Ferguson, *The Aquarian Conspiracy* (Los Angeles: J. P. Tarcher, 1980), 38.
6. Thomas Ryan, *Wellness, Spirituality and Sports* (New York: Paulist Press, 1986), 38.
7. Ann McGee-Cooper et al., *You Don't Have to Go Home from Work Exhausted!* (New York: Bantam Books, 1992), 176.

CHAPTER 7. CONTRIBUTE TO AN EFFECTIVE WORK COMMUNITY

Epigraph: Marvin R. Weisbord, *Productive Workplaces* (San Francisco: Jossey-Bass, 1987), 1.

1. Robert Levering, *A Great Place to Work* (New York: Random House, 1988).
2. John Naisbitt and Patricia Aburdene, *Re-inventing the Corporation* (New York: Warner, 1985).
3. Peter M. Senge, *The Fifth Discipline* (New York: Currency/Doubleday, 1990), 14.

4. Naisbitt and Aburdene, *Re-inventing the Corporation*, 21.
5. Naisbitt and Aburdene, *Re-inventing the Corporation*, 22.
6. Senge, *The Fifth Discipline*, 140.
7. Ross West, *How to Be Happier in the Job You Sometimes Can't Stand* (Nashville: Broadman Press, 1990), 30.
8. West, *How to Be Happier*, 31.
9. West, *How to Be Happier*, 115.
10. West, *How to Be Happier*, 115.
11. Max DePree, *Leadership Jazz* (New York: Currency/Doubleday, 1992); Max DePree, *Leadership Is an Art* (East Lansing: Michigan Univ. Press, 1987).
12. DePree, *Leadership Jazz*, 102-3.
13. DePree, *Leadership Is an Art*, 27.
14. DePree, *Leadership Is an Art*, 55-56.
15. Barbara Cooney, *Miss Rumphius* (New York: Puffin Books, 1982). The quoted phrase comes from this passage in Cooney's delightful children's book:

    In the evening Alice sat on her grandfather's knee and listened to his stories of faraway places. When he had finished, Alice would say, "When I grow up, I too will go to faraway places, and when I grow old, I too will live beside the sea."
    "That is all very well, little Alice," said her grandfather, "but there is a third thing you must do."
    "What is that?" asked Alice. "You must do something to make the world more beautiful," said her grandfather.
16. DePree, *Leadership Jazz*, 162.
17. Weisbord, *Productive Workplaces*, 265-66.

CHAPTER 8. CREATE YOUR BEST WORK

Epigraph: Carolyn Jabs, "How to Kick a Dream into Action," *Self*, May 1986, 122.

1. Robert Fritz, *The Path of Least Resistance: Learning to Become the Creative Force in Your Own Life* (New York: Fawcett Columbine, 1989).
2. Marvin R. Weisbord, *Productive Workplaces* (San Francisco: Jossey-Bass, 1987). Chapter describes his future search process. This is further elaborated in Weisbord's later book *Discovering Common Ground* (Philadelphia: Blue Sky Productions, 1992).
3. Ram Dass, "Is Enlightenment Good for Your Mental Health?" *The Common Boundary* 6, no. 5 (September/October 1988), 8.
4. The Giraffe Project, P.O. Box 759, Langley Whidbey Island, WA 98260.
5. *The Giraffe Gazette* 4, no. 4 (Summer/Fall 1988), 8, 9.
6. John Graham, "Celebrating Success," *The Giraffe Gazette* 4, no. 4 (Summer/Fall 1988), 9.
7. Graham, "Celebrating Success," 12-13.
8. Graham, "Celebrating Success," 13.

APPENDIX D

1. Ann McGee-Cooper, *You Don't Have to Go Home from Work Exhausted!* (New York: Bantam Books, 1992), 232.

Suggested Reading

Books We Have Found Most Useful Over the Years

Anderson, Sherry R., and Patricia Hopkins. *The Feminine Face of God.* New York: Bantam Books, 1991. Through interviews with spiritually mature women, the authors show how women have redefined traditional beliefs and rediscovered their own spiritual heritage.

Anzalone, Joan, ed. *Good Works: A Guide to Careers in Social Change.* New York: Dembner Books, 1985. Profiles of individuals working for social change, plus a listing of relevant organizations and resources.

Berkowitz, Bill. *Local Heroes.* Lexington, MA: Lexington Books, 1987. Portraits of twenty people who have made a difference in grass-roots America. If they can do it, so can we!

Bolles, Richard Nelson. *What Color Is Your Parachute?* Berkeley, CA: Ten Speed Press, republished annually. A useful compendium of information for job hunters and career changers.

Bracey, Hyler, and Jack Rosenblum, Aubrey Sanford, and Roy Trueblood. *Managing from the Heart.* New York: Delacorte Press, 1990. A parable about how one driven manager becomes a caring, compassionate leader.

Campbell, David, Ph.D. *If You Don't Know Where You're Going, You'll Probably End Up Somewhere Else.* Allen, TX: Argus Communications, 1974. Especially written for young people, this book helps you raise and address the big questions of what to do in life and how to find help.

Covey, Stephen R. *Principle-Centered Leadership.* New York: Simon & Schuster, 1992. Personal and organizational strategies to produce top-notch work.

DePree, Max. *Leadership Jazz.* New York: Currency/Doubleday, 1992. Essays from a seasoned CEO on how to make the workplace run with harmony.

Ferguson, Marilyn. *The Aquarian Conspiracy.* Los Angeles: J. P. Tarcher, 1980. Inspiring cultural analysis of trends in personal and social transformation.

Fox, Matthew. *Creation Spirituality.* San Francisco: San Francisco, 1991. A contemporary spirituality relevant to our multicultural existence and based on ancient and modern wisdom.

Harman, Willis, and John Hormann. *Creative Work.* Indianapolis, IN: Knowledge Systems, 1990. New ways of doing business that will engage people's creativity in building a viable future.

Keen, Sam. *The Passionate Life: Stages of Loving.* San Francisco: Harper & Row, 1983. Stages in developing the capacity to love: the child, adult, rebel, outlaw, and lover/fool.

May, Gerald G. *The Awakened Heart.* San Francisco: HarperSanFrancisco, 1991. Integrating the wisdom of psychology, ancient and contemporary spiritual practices, and personal experience, May explores ways of tapping into the love we all desire.

May, Rollo. *The Courage to Create.* New York: Bantam Books, 1975. A brief but powerful discussion of creativity—how it works, how it feels, how to cultivate this "healthiest impulse."

McGee-Cooper, Ann, with Duane Trammell and Barbara Lau. *You Don't Have to Go Home from Work Exhausted!* Dallas, TX: Bowen & Rogers, 1990. A guide for energizing your work habits, thinking patterns, work environment, evening and weekend playtime, and overall approach to life.

McMakin, Jacqueline, and Rhoda Nary. *The Doorways Series.* San Francisco: HarperSan Francisco, 1993. Four guides that offer a faith perspective on discovering gifts and life purpose: "Encountering God in the Old Testament," "Meeting Jesus in the New Testament," "Journeying with the Spirit," "Discovering Your Gifts, Vision, and Call." A practical approach, including activities to do alone and with others.

Miller, Luree. *Late Bloom.* New York: Paddington Press, 1979. Stories of how women have changed their lives, careers, and relationships, a celebration of those who also have decided to "live according to their talents."

Moore, Thomas. *Care of the Soul.* New York: Harper Collins, 1992. How to add spirituality, depth, and meaning to modern-day life by nurturing the soul.

Moran, Peg. *Invest in Yourself.* Garden City, NY: Doubleday, 1983. How to start your own business, plus interviews with thirteen people who have done it.

Naisbitt, John, and Patricia Aburdene. *Re-inventing the Corporation.* New York: Warner Books, 1985. Trends, guidelines, and examples that inspire us to create workplaces where people and profits can flourish.

Parker, Yana. *The Damn Good Résumé Guide.* Berkeley, CA: Ten Speed Press, 1986. Our most-used résumé guide. Great on one-page résumés. We would not be without it.

Phifer, Paul. *College Majors and Careers: A Resource for Effective Life Planning.* Garrett Park, MD: Garrett Park Press, 1987. A handy directory that lists fields of interest, related occupations, relevant avocational and leisure-time activities, related skills, sources for further exploration.

Robbins, Lois. *Waking Up in the Age of Creativity.* Santa Fe, NM: Bear & Company, 1985. Specific practical ways to free up and foster creativity in all aspects of life.

Rosen, Robert H., with Lisa Berger. *The Healthy Company.* New York: Jeremy P. Tarcher/Perigee Books, 1991. How to be your own CEO who can personalize and institutionalize what it takes to produce excellent work in healthy organizations.

Senge, Peter M. *The Fifth Discipline.* New York: Doubleday/Currency, 1990. How to create a learning organization that contributes to the wellness of the planet.

Sher, Barbara, and Annie Gottlieb. *Teamworks!* New York: Warner Books, 1989. How to run "success teams" that help each member actualize dreams.

Sinetar, Marsha. *A Way Without Words.* New York: Paulist Press, 1992. Step-by-step guide for cultivating personal spirituality.

———. *Do What You Love, the Money Will Follow.* Mahwah, NJ: Paulist Press, 1987. A guide to overcoming obstacles to doing the work you love.

Weisbord, Marvin. *Productive Workplaces: Organizing and Managing for Dignity, Meaning and Community.* How to create workplaces where people learn and grow as they cooperate to improve an organization's performance.

West, Ross. *How to Be Happier in the Job You Sometimes Can't Stand.* Nashville: Broadman Press, 1990. A practical pick-me-up for anyone with the job blues.

About the Authors

Jacqueline McMakin and Sonya Dyer met 25 years ago during their involvement in interracial work in the Washington, DC, area. Since then, they have sought to overcome barriers and open closed doors for themselves and others.

Sparked by a commitment to create new ways to live and work and to pass on the tools that had been useful to them in vocational development, they established the nonprofit organization Working from the Heart. Its purpose is to help people explore the role of meaning in their lives and to discern how to express that through work. Through their nine-month seminar, the Life Direction Lab, and through shorter workshops, Sonya and Jackie use psychological, career development, and spiritual tools to help people articulate life direction and develop a vocation that honors the totality of their lives. They emphasize the importance of "mutual mentoring," people helping each other find what they are looking for.

Their vision is that everyone have the opportunity to do worthwhile work. Our interconnected world requires that all of us pull together toward developing a society that works. One of the ways to do that is to find work that really needs doing and put our heart and soul into giving it our best. To help foster this vision, Sonya and Jackie invite each of us to spread the word that

1. Meaningful work is an essential building block of a healthy society and something everyone can learn how to find or develop.

2. Mutual mentoring is a tool that can be learned and used to help each of us develop meaningful work.

3. Small mutual mentoring groups in companies, schools, churches, and communities can be the vehicles through which people support each other to offer their best.

4. The eight steps to meaningful work as described in this book provide basic content that can help each person move toward the work they really want to do.

In addition to her work as co-director of Working from the Heart, Jackie is the author with Rhoda Nary of the *Doorways Series*, four guides that offer a faith perspective on discovering gifts and life purpose, also published by Harper San Francisco. A vocational counselor and organizational consultant, she holds an M.A. in theology from The Catholic University of America.

Sonya is the leader of the pastoral team of the Seekers Community, Church of the Saviour, Washington, DC. A trained social worker, she works directly with urban homeless families through For Love of Children (FLOC).

Both authors are also available for training and consultation. Reach them at 1309 Merchant Lane, McLean, VA 22101. (703) 827-0336 Tuesday and Thursday only.

Index

Aburdene, Patricia, 133, 134
Age, parameters of, 63
Aldridge, Earl Zela, 162
Aquarian Conspiracy (Ferguson), 121

Barron, Frank, 73
Bellah, Robert, 47–48
Best work, 2, 3, 149–66; balanced with rest of life, 160–62; celebrating, 162–63; and community, 132; creating, 53–54, 152–60; embodying, 53–54; exercises, 152, 156–57, 160, 162, 163; Gathering, 164–65
Black, Shirley Temple, 102
Bliss, following, 23–27, 96
Block, Peter, 53–54
Boucher, Norman, 55
Brain hemispheres, 6
Buddha, 33
Burnout, cure for, 181–82

Calling, 43–47
Campbell, Joseph, 11, 23, 96, 118–19
Care, gift of, 28–29
Celebration: of best work, 162–63, 165; heart of, 41
Christman Brothers, 54
City of Joy (Lapierre), 114
Communities: as meaning source, 47–49. *See also* Work community
Compassion: gift of, 28–29; heart of, 41
Corrigan, Meirad, 44
Covenant, in work community, 147
Creativity, 6, 16; best work, 53–54, 152–60; heart of, 40; and nourishment, 116–20; vs. reactive mode, 152; in work community, 146–47
Credentialing, training for, 175

Cuomo, Mario, 36

DePree, Max, 146–47
Do What You Love, The Money Will Follow (Sinetar), 32
Dreams. *See* Vocational dreams

Education: continuing, 83; experiences through, 40, 83. *See also* Training
Empowered Manager (Block), 53–54
Exercises, 5–6; best work, 152, 156–57, 160, 162, 163; gifts, 14–15, 17–18, 21–22, 25–27, 29–30, 33–34; meaning, 39, 42–43, 46–47, 48–49, 51, 54; nourishment, 116, 118–20, 122–23, 125–26, 127, 130; parameters, 57, 58–64, 65–66, 67–68, 72; people help, 95–96, 97–101, 104, 105–7, 108–9, 111; vocational dreams, 76, 77–78, 83, 85, 87, 91; work community, 133, 137, 139–40, 142, 144, 148. *See also* Gatherings
Experience: education, 40, 83; and gifts, 13; and meaning, 39–43; and vocational dreams, 79, 82–83, 86, 89–90; work, 41, 82

Failure: creativity and, 16; recognition of, 163
Faith: calling received through, 44; experiences through, 40–41
Family, experiences through, 40
Ferguson, Marilyn, 44, 121
Fifth Discipline (Senge), 81, 133
Focusing, 2, 57, 152–57
Fowler, James, 120
Fox, Matthew, 40–41
Freud, Sigmund, 45, 46
Fritz, Robert, 152–56, 158, 161, 163

Gatherings, 6–9; best work, 164–65; gifts, 30–31; meaning, 51–53; nourishment, 128–29; parameters, 69–71; people help, 109–10; vocational dreams, 87–89; work community, 145–46

Gifts, 2, 11–34; best work and, 151; calling received through, 44; exercises, 14–15, 17–18, 21–22, 25–27, 29–30, 33–34; field guide to, 12–15; following bliss, 23–27; Gathering, 30–31; of heart, 28–29; and moneymaking, 32–34; of soul, 28–29; and vocational dreams, 74–75; and work community, 134; workout for, 27–30. *See also* Creativity

Gill-Austern, Brita L., 35
Giraffe Project, 162
Goodman, Ellen, 58
Graham, John, 162, 163
Great Place to Work (Levering), 133
Grief, experiences through, 41–42
Group, 5, 6–9. *See also* Gatherings

Habits of the Heart (Bellah et al.), 47–48
Haldane, Bernard, 23–24
Hartke, Gilbert, 94
Health, parameters of, 56, 63
Heart: of compassion/justice-making/healing/celebration, 41; of creativity, 40; of exaltation, 40; gift of, 28–29; journey of, 40–41; of silence, 40
Help. *See* People help
"How to Kick a Dream into Action" (Jabs), 65

Information: from associations, 81; concrete, 169–70; interviewing for, 80–81, 169–74; in libraries, 81
Inner Companions (McCarthy), 105
In Search of Our Mothers' Gardens (Walker), 95
Interviewing: evaluation, 172–73; execution, 171–73; feelings and, 170; follow-up, 173; for information, 80–81, 169–74; preparation, 170–71; training leaders, 177; write-up, 173–74, 179

Jabs, Carolyn, 65, 149

Job dissatisfaction factors, 142–43
"Jobless at 61: A Success Story" (Van Sickle), 107–8
Job satisfaction factors, 143
Josefowitz, Natasha, 93
Jung, C. G., 44, 45–46

Keen, Sam, 120
Keller, Helen, 94–95
Kennedy, Ted, Jr., 56
Key life factors, 129–30
Kovalski, Stephan, 114

Lapierre, Dominique, 114
Leadership Is an Art (DePree), 146
Leadership Jazz (DePree), 146
LeMond, Greg, 152–53
Levering, Robert, 133
Libraries, information in, 81
Life Direction Labs, 4
Life Maps (Fowler & Keen), 120
Life/Stage: key life factors, 129–30; parameters of, 63
Limitations, 56–57
Location, parameters of, 62
Luce, Clare Boothe, 102

McCarthy, Colman, 105
McGee-Cooper, Ann, 129–30
Macy, Joanna, 38
Madeira School, 132
Managing from the Heart, 28–29
Mandalas, 45–46
May, Rollo, 116
Meaning, 2, 35–54; best work and, 151; calling, 43–47; community as source of, 47–49; essence, 49–51; exercises, 39, 42–43, 46–47, 48–49, 51, 54; experienced, 39–43; Gathering, 51–53; passion, 38; stew, 50; and vision, 38, 44, 53–54; and vocational dreams, 74–75; and work community, 134
Medlock, Anne, 162
Mentoring, mutual, 24–25
Mentors, 96, 98
Money needs: and doing what you love, 32–34, 167–68; parameters of, 56

Index

Moore, Thomas, 28
Moyers, Bill, 23
Murray, Margo, 96
Mysticism, 121

Naisbitt, John, 133, 134
Networks, people, 95, 111
Nourishment, 2, 113–30; body, 124; combinations, 123–26; creativity and, 116–20; daily, 126–27; energy flow, 129–30; exercises, 116, 118–20, 122–23, 125–26, 127, 130; Gathering, 128–29; in-the-moment, 127; mind, 124; mystery and, 120–23; planned, 127; roots and wings, 124; spirit, 124; transcendence and, 120–23; and work community, 135–36

O'Connor, Elizabeth, 67
Our Many Selves (O'Connor), 67
Outlaw self, 120

Pain, experiences through, 41–42
Parameters, 2, 55–72; best work and, 151; busting loose, 64–66; dragon slaying, 66–68; exercises, 57, 58–64, 65–66, 67–68, 72; fixed, 68–69; Gathering, 69–71; inventory, 58–64; lack of, 57; limitations, 56–57; survey, 71–72; and vocational dreams, 74–75; and work community, 134–35
Partner, 6–9. *See also* Gatherings
Passion, 2, 38
Pathfinders (Sheehy), 36
Path of Least Resistance (Fritz), 152
Paul, Saint, 66
People help, 2, 93–111; adviser, 98–99; best work and, 151; collaborator, 99; colleague, 97; exercises, 95–96, 97–101, 104, 105–7, 108–9, 111; friend, 100; Gathering, 109–10; inside, 104–7; inventory, 97–101; mentor, 96, 98; patron, 100–101; role model, 99; spiritual guide, 101; supervisor, 98; teacher, 100; and work community, 135
Philosophy, experiences through, 40–41
Playfulness, 6, 16

Poetry, 119, 120
Practical Parameters Inventory, 58–64

Ram Dass, 159
Reactive mode, 152
Re-inventing the Corporation (Naisbitt & Aburdene), 133
Relationships, parameters of, 63–64
Resource myopia, 16
Rewards, parameters of, 60–62
Robbins, Lois, 16, 118
Roszak, Theodore, 113
Rumi, 151
Ryan, Thomas, 124

Schweickart, Russell, 41
Selves, 67; altruistic, 67; changing, 142–44; keep-up-with-the-Joneses, 67; outlaw, 120; reflective, 78; spontaneous, 78
Senge, Peter M., 81, 133, 135
Sheehy, Gail, 36
Sher, Barbara, 81
Sinetar, Marsha, 32, 33
Skills: gift as, 13; training for, 175
Smith, Joan, 21
Social context, experiences through, 41
Sommers, Tish, 84
Soul: gift of, 28–29; sustaining, 114–16
Success: celebrating, 162–63; in communities, 48
Sullivan, Annie, 95

Tennen, Laura, 55
Terkel, Studs, v, 43–44
Thomas, Bruce, 38–39
Time: management of, 160–61; parameters of, 59–60
Training: decisions about, 175–79; experiences from, 82–83. *See also* Education

Van Sickle, Carol, 107–8
Vision: of greatness, 53–54; meaning and, 38, 44, 53–54; quest, 120–23; reality tension with, 153–54, 156–57; of vocational dreams, 153–57, 161; in work community, 134
Vocation, 43–47

Vocational dreams, 2, 73-91; best work and, 151; bugaboos, 76-77; exercises, 76, 77-78, 83, 85, 87, 91; experience, 79, 82-83, 86, 89-90; exploring, 76-87, 89-90; Gathering, 87-89; listening to, 89-91; reading, 79, 81, 86, 89-90; talking, 79-81, 86, 89-90; visioning, 153-57, 161; and work community, 135

Vocation Exploration Plans, 84-87

Waking Up in the Age of Creativity (Robbins), 16, 118
Walker, Alice, 95, 153
Watson, Nora, v, 43-44
Weisbord, Marvin R., 131, 148, 155
Wellness, Spirituality, and Sports (Ryan), 124
West, Ross, 142-43
Wishcraft (Sher), 81

Work: dissatisfaction/satisfaction, 142-43; experience, 41, 82; internship, 82; parttime, 82; temporary, 82; transition, 167-68; vacation, 82. *See also* Best work

Work community, 2-3, 131-48; arenas for change, 141; change-making actions, 138-42; change yourself, 142-44; climate for change, 146-48; covenant, 147; creativity, 146-47; direction of change, 138; exercises, 133, 137, 139-40, 142, 144, 148; Gathering, 145-46; ideal and reality, 133-37; job satisfaction/dissatisfaction, 142-43; mandate change, 138; model change, 138; plan change, 138; request change, 138; stimulate change, 138

Working (Terkel), v, 43-44
Workshops, 82-83, 135

Printed in the United States
70801LV00004B/29-38